Groans of the Spirit

Princeton Theological Monograph Series

K. C. Hanson, Charles M. Collier, D. Christopher Spinks,
and Robin Parry, Series Editors

Recent volumes in the series:

Nicholaus Ludwig von Zinzendorf
Christian Life and Witness: Count Zinzendorf's 1738 Berlin Speeches

Donald E. Gowan
The Bible on Forgiveness

Hemchand Gossai
Power and Marginality in the Abraham Narrative—Second Edition

Myk Habets
The Anointed Son: A Trinitarian Spirit Christology

Christopher L. Fisher
*Human Significance in Theology and the Natural Sciences:
An Ecumenical Perspective with Reference to Pannenberg,
Rahner, and Zizioulas*

William A. Tooman
*Transforming Visions: Transformations of Text, Tradition,
and Theology in Ezekiel*

William J. Meyer
*Metaphysics and the Future of Theology: The Voice of Theology
in Public Life*

David H. Nikkel
Radical Embodiment

Groans of the Spirit

Homiletical Dialectics in an Age of Confusion

TIMOTHY MATTHEW SLEMMONS

PICKWICK *Publications* · Eugene, Oregon

GROANS OF THE SPIRIT
Homiletical Dialectics in an Age of Confusion

Princeton Theological Monograph Series 138

Pickwick Publications
An Imprint of Wipf and Stock Publishers
199 W. 8th Ave., Suite 3
Eugene, OR 97401

www.wipfandstock.com

ISBN 13: 978-1-60608-904-0

Cataloging-in-Publication data

Slemmons, Timothy Matthew.

    Groans of the spirit : homiletical dialectics in an age of confusion / Timothy Matthew Slemmons.

    Princeton Theological Monograph Series 138

    xiv + 140 p. ; 23 cm. —Includes bibliographical references and indexes.

    ISBN 13: 978-1-60608-904-0

    1. Preaching. 2. Barth, Karl, 1886–1855. 3. Kierkegaard, Soren, 1813–1855. I. Title. II. Series.

BV4211.2 S565 2010

In grateful memory of my loving father
and the most joyful man I have ever known
Robert Sheldon Slemmons
(1922–2007)

While I kept silence, my body wasted away
through my groaning all day long. (Ps 32:3)

The roads to Zion mourn,
for no one comes to the festivals;
all her gates are desolate,
her priests groan;
her young girls grieve,
and her lot is bitter. (Lam 1:4)

Likewise the Spirit helps us in our weakness; for we do not know
how to pray as we ought, but that very Spirit intercedes with sighs
too deep for words. (Rom 8:26)

For while we are still in this tent, we groan under our burden,
because we wish not to be unclothed but to be further clothed, so
that what is mortal may be swallowed up by life. (2 Cor 5:3–4)

Contents

Acknowledgments

As I have often said to the congregations I have served, it is an exceedingly good thing that the Gospel promises us eternal life, for many reasons, obviously, but not least among them is the fact that we finite creatures, having received literally countless gifts and graces from the infinite, eternal, Triune God, will need all of eternity to worship and give thanks to God accordingly. This statement alone, framed in view of the "infinite qualitative difference" that is the focus of much of this little book, will attest that the present list of acknowledgements should be inestimably longer than space will allow, as should the book itself, which attestation will be clear enough if the reader receives it aright, namely, as a deep sigh of longing to be faithful in preaching and to discover new friends who likewise seek to be faithful in preaching and who likewise understand such faithfulness as the chief expression of thanksgiving to God for the Gospel itself, which is "the power of God for salvation to everyone who has faith" (Rom 1:16).

But grace itself sees to it that "*Soli Deo Gloria!*" invites elaboration. Thus, I wish to give particular thanks to James F. Kay of Princeton Theological Seminary who willingly bore with my laborious upbringing in my doctoral studies, especially with my Kierkegaardian verbosity in "writing in order to learn." Jim Kay is renowned among his students as a gracious, generous, and discerning reader, as well as a meticulous editor and proofreader; in many ways, Jim is the premiere theologian of preaching working today. Without bearing any responsibility for the fouls I may have committed and the faults I may have introduced into these chapters, Jim's tutelage occasioned the drafting of the first two of these chapters during my PhD studies, and his feedback at the time made them incalculably better than they would have been otherwise.

I also wish to thank Cleophus J. LaRue, also of Princeton Seminary, for assigning me the task of lecturing on preaching. Although at the time, I had no idea how distant would be the prospect of lecturing to anyone on anything, the "imagined occasion" of this lecture on the content of Christian proclamation (chapter 3) afforded me the freedom to distill much of what I had been formulating regarding what I take to be the non-negotiable and inescapable dialectics that are ever at work as we preach amidst the endless negotiations that characterize the fields of contextual studies and the dogged and often tiresome claims of hermeneutics.

Thanks are due as well to my teachers and colleagues at Princeton Seminary for many rich interactions at the time: Charles L. Bartow, Sally A. Brown, Michael Brothers, Nancy Lammers-Gross, David A. Davis, Kenyatta Gilbert, Peter Henry, Charles "Chip" Hardwick, Angela Hancock, and Shauna Hannan. My studies with the late James E. Loder, Princeton's resident Kierkegaardian, were especially delightful, "a pearl of great price." The First Presbyterian Church, Titusville, NJ, was especially generous in allowing me time to teach in an adjunct capacity at Princeton Seminary and to make good use of the pastor's study in the years that followed my doctoral work.

Further, I am inexpressibly grateful to and for my new colleagues at the University of Dubuque Theological Seminary (UDTS), especially President Jeffrey Bullock, himself a Gadamerian, whose conversational and pastoral approach to preaching, ministry, and the mission of the university mitigates to a considerable degree the concerns I express in these pages with regard to his favored theorist of philosophical hermeneutics and speaks much better of Gadamer's influence than I am capable of doing; Dean Bradley Longfield and Associate Dean Richard "Skip" Shaffer, whose collegiality and administrative oversight cultivate a remarkable and rare ethos of *koinonia* among the faculty, staff, and students, and who were each instrumental in calling me to UDTS; as well as David Moessner, Rob Hoch, and Gary Neal Hansen (UDTS), and Robert Reid (University of Dubuque), each of whom have engaged me in conversation in gracious ways and at various times, if not directly with regard to the present material, then on the general subjects treated here. I also wish to express my appreciation for Beth McCaw (UDTS), Tammy Weins-Sorge (General Assembly Council), and the 2009–11 cohort of DMin students at UDTS, for modeling a spiritual and intellectual fellowship of pastor/scholars for which many in ministry often express great hunger and for the lack of which many pastors and congregations suffer tremendously; the receptivity of this group and all the students at UDTS (regardless of their program) to the concerns, the "homiletical dialectics," in evidence here are of enormous encouragement to me, and I am grateful for each of them.

I would also be remiss if I failed to acknowledge the cordial collegiality of George W. Stroup (Columbia Seminary) who long ago not only introduced me to Gadamer's thought, but also directed my growing interest in Kierkegaard toward the Dane's Christological writings. This was a most providential turn for which I remain exceedingly grateful. Walter Brueggemann has been an ongoing source of inspiration and benevolent provocation for two decades now, yet what relatively few of his readers realize is that his faithfulness as a gracious correspondent and supporter of his students exceeds even his breathtaking productivity; that he has willingly read and recommended this modest volume entails no small "stoop," yet another one, on his part. I also continue to treasure many formative lessons from my first instructors of preaching at Columbia Seminary, the late Lucy A. Rose and Charles L. (Chuck) Campbell (now at Duke), not least the encouraging tone and the pastoral ethos they established in delivering feedback on student sermons. Theirs is a model I continue to aspire to emulate.

On a more personal note, I must express my profound thanks to and for my wife Victoria, for her unfailing support and faithfulness as we together have prayerfully sought my development as a preacher and a teacher of preaching. The prayers of Barbara Suppe and Barbara Matlack have also been instrumental, as have been those of Victoria's late mother, Barbara W. Smith, who always took a keen interest in my work. Other members of Victoria's family and my own, especially Karen and Ashley Smith, C. Michael and Jennifer Kuner, Claire and Bob Forster, Rob Slemmons and Julie Devoe, have each been consistently warm and supportive in their unique ways. My own parents, now temporarily separated by death after sixty-two years of marriage, deserve thanks and acknowledgment for embodying the "steadfast love of the LORD" in such a way as to make a straight path for their children's faith in the goodness of God. The imperative for upholding the "infinite qualitative difference" notwithstanding, if there were ever two people from whose manner of living one might analogously infer and inform one's understanding of and belief in the love of God, it is my mother and my late father, to whom this book is joyfully dedicated.

Abbreviations

AHD   *The American Heritage Dictionary, Second College Edition.* Boston: Houghton Mifflin, 1982.

BO   *The Constitution of the Presbyterian Church (U.S.A.). Part II—Book of Order (2009–2011).* Louisville: The Office of the General Assembly, 2009.

CD   *Church Dogmatics, Vols. 1–4.* Karl Barth. Edited and translated by G. W. Bromiley and T. F. Torrance. Edinburgh: T. & T. Clark, 1936–1958.

CEP   *Concise Encyclopedia of Preaching.* Edited by William H. Willimon and Richard Lischer. Louisville: Westminster John Knox, 1995.

CRDT   *Karl Barth's Critically Realistic Dialectical Theology: Its Genesis and Development 1909–1936.* Bruce McCormack. Oxford: Clarendon, 1995.

DGD   *The Göttingen Dogmatics. Instruction in the Christian Religion,* Vol. 1. *Karl Barth.* Grand Rapids: Eerdmans, 1991.

ERF   *Encyclopedia of the Reformed Faith.* Edited by Donald K. McKim. Louisville: Westminster John Knox, 1992.

JP   *Søren Kierkegaard's Journals and Papers.* 7 vols. Edited and translated by Howard V. Hong and Edna H. Hong. Bloomington: Indiana University Press, 1967–1978.

KW   *Kierkegaard's Writings.* 26 vols. Series edited by Howard V. and Edna H. Hong. Princeton, NJ: Princeton University Press, 1978–2000.

LW   *Luther's Works.* 55 vols. Edited by Jaroslav Pelikan and
         Helmut T. Lehman. Philadelphia: Fortress; St. Louis:
         Concordia, 1955–1986.

OCP   *The Oxford Companion to Philosophy.* Edited by Ted
         Honderich. Oxford: Oxford University Press, 1995.

TM   *Truth and Method.* Hans-Georg Gadamer. Translated by
         Joel Weinsheimer and Donald G. Marshall. New York:
         Continuum, 1997.

WGWM   *The Word of God and the Word of Man.* Karl Barth.
         Translated by Douglas Horton. Gloucester, MA: Peter
         Smith, 1928.

Introduction

THE PRESENT VOLUME OF TWO ESSAYS, ONE "DISCOURSE ON AN IMAG-
ined occasion," and two sermons on "the narrow gate," proceeds from
such a lengthy list of concerns, one can scarcely hope it will succeed
in much more than registering these concerns and explaining whence
they arise. Permit me to begin with the latter.

At its most basic, developmental level, the main part of this book
is simply a compilation of projects (chapters 1 through 3) that emerged
during my doctoral studies at Princeton Seminary, each of which bears
close relation to my unpublished dissertation dealing with Kierkegaard's
theology and practice of preaching.[1] Although these essays were not
included in that dissertation, they developed concurrently with it, and
constitute (to my mind) a modest down payment, "the earnest"—to
employ the Jacobean rendering relating to the gift of "the Holy Spirit of
promise" (Eph 1:13–14)—that I would apply to the commitment I made
there, in the final chapter, in which I enumerated ten "normative criteria
for a qualitatively penitential homiletic."

These normative criteria, each of which will be in evidence here,
are: (1) a dialectical (Kierkegaardian/Barthian) epistemology that
takes stock of the "infinite qualitative difference" between the existential spheres; (2) the Christological content of Christian proclamation;
(3) a restatement of "the unity of preaching" as obtaining not in terms
of form and content, but between content, authority, and unity itself
(characterized by the work of the Holy Spirit) within the sphere of faith;
(4) a retrieval of direct address in preaching; (5) the need to preserve
the individual-communal dialectic in the use of direct address; (6) the
importance of Kierkegaard's concept of contemporaneity (understood
in terms of the kerygmatic real presence of Christ and the Holy Spirit)
for prayer and for preaching with direct address; (7) the function of
directness in dialectic (often simplistically characterized as inherently

1. Slemmons, "Toward a Penitential Homiletic."

indirect); (8) a restatement of Kierkegaard's theory of "indirect communication" (as it applies to preaching) in terms of indicative ethics; (9) the essentially upbuilding, i.e., loving, nature of preaching according to a penitential homiletic; and (10) the claim that a penitential, homiletical dialectic is not a syncretistic Both/And, or a decision-istic Either/Or, but a *qualitative* From/To.

That is a dense list of criteria that emerged painstakingly in the aforementioned work, so I will not elaborate upon them here, except to alert the reader to the fact that they are never far from view in the present book. Although I believe they merit further development elsewhere, three of these criteria do receive more focused attention here than do the others: first, the "infinite qualitative difference," in dealing Karl Barth's dialectic (chapter 1); second, contemporaneity, in my critique of Gadamer and of the inherently mythical implications of hermeneutics more generally (chapter 2); and third, the Christological content of preaching (chapter 3).

To further enlarge upon this assemblage of essays on homiletically-concerned dialectics, what I wish to retain from both Kierkegaard and Barth, what both thinkers have to offer, is a model of reading scripture in a dialectically penetrating way, a way that depends on (1) the exegete's taking seriously the problem of theological anthropology; as well as, (2) the prayerful *epiclesis*, the referral of interpretation to the God-man, Jesus Christ, as the ultimate referent for revealed Truth; (3) a venture or a leap of faith that involves a double and dialectical conviction of one's own sin, on the one hand, and of the grace of God toward oneself and the world, those who languish under the burden of sin, on the other; and (4) the recognition that this conviction, while it occurs in real, historical time, involves the same God-man, who, through the "earnest" of the Holy Spirit, is present and available "in time" and "from eternity" to come to the aid of the temporal creature, giving understanding, encouragement, and faith. Thus, these essays attempt to reclaim and show the rehabilitating power of the Spirit in an age of confusion as it is perceived and described by dialectical *theology*, an age in which dialectical thinking has been and is still very much abused.

The particular problem to which they apply themselves, with increasing directness, is "the content of Christian proclamation." For it is in refocusing on the Christological content of preaching, on the work and the person and the prototype of Christ Jesus, not first on the soteriological *results* of his work, his person, his teaching, or his "example," that the preacher, the listener, the reader of scripture, and the church, all stand to gain a fresh perspective on the glory, and on the believer's proper enjoyment, of the Triune God.

In the first essay, I seek to clarify what is at stake in a proper understanding of (theological) dialectics.[2] Here I rely on two recent contributions to Barth scholarship, namely, those of Daniel Migliore and Bruce McCormack, in order to get at the key dialectics at work in Barth's thought, and how these relate (dialectically!) to analogical thinking. Although one is hard-pressed to differentiate cleanly between, for instance, Barth's dialectical method, the dialectic of contradictory human existence, and the dialectic of revelation and hiddenness, as each impinges profoundly on the other, what does arise is a clear realization that an honest engagement with the full breadth of scriptural revelation and with the centrality of revelation in the God-man requires that one not cling to one biblical concept or its opposite, but enter into the multidimensional and multifarious tensions at work therein, even while one expects in faith an asymmetrical pressure to arise and drive one in the direction of one (N.B. or the other!) of these opposing forces. Because it seems to me that the soteriological presuppositions and the exaggerated priority placed upon ethics (as divorced from a robust doctrine of the agency of the God-man in human transformation) that both lie behind the present state of affairs are best exposed in light of the dialectic of eternity and temporality, a dialectic that is sadly neglected in almost every field of mainline theological scholarship today—consider, for instance, the one-sidedly temporal nature of gender, narrative, literary, and historical studies; and because Barth most clearly associates Kierkegaard with his own articulation of this dialectic, I apply this "infinite qualitative difference" in the analysis of two critiques of Barth's

2. By "theological" dialectics, I have in mind not merely the premiere theologians who have come to be associated with dialectical theology, but also a radically scriptural distinction between the New Testament terms *dialegesthai*, on the one hand, and *dialogizesthai* (v.) /*dialogismos* (n.), on the other. See chapter 1, §2.4, below. What I expressly do not intend is any reference to Hegelian dialectical philosophy, Marxist socioeconomic theory, or neo-Marxist critical theory. "Critical" as a Christian understanding of homiletical dialectics may be, what one gains from Kierkegaard on this score is the clarifying teleology at the heart of his dialectic and the essentially *agapic* character of homiletic, especially in evidence in his discourse: "Love Builds Up," in *Works of Love*, 209–24. (It goes without saying this has nothing whatsoever to do with the "negative dialectics" of Theodore W. Adorno, perhaps the most notorious mis-interpreter of Kierkegaard on record.)

homiletical thought, those of David Buttrick and Ruthanna B. Hooke. Finally, I propose a pedagogical exercise in which the speeches of Jesus in the Gospel of Mark are investigated as statements in which this dialectic is presupposed and the reader/hearer is therefore ideally conditioned (if one can put it this way) to encounter the Christological revelation, that is, within a clarification of the crisis of theological anthropology. In short, the infinite difference itself is not the content of preaching, but a necessary and suitable description of every status quo—all cultural and historical particularities notwithstanding—that the preaching of God's Word must address.

In the second essay, I offer a critical comparison of Kierkegaard's Christo-pneumatic concept of contemporaneity with the handling of this concept in the hermeneutical thought of Hans-Georg Gadamer. Here again, in the temporal-eternal dialectic, which is in a certain sense synonymous with contemporaneity in Kierkegaard, one sees the qualitative qualification (so to speak) that Kierkegaard gives it gets lost when Gadamer drops contemporaneity into the lower existential sphere of esthetics and confuses eternity with temporal endurance. In order to try and reestablish the qualitative distinction, I suggest that the etymological presupposition and the mythical analogy that lurk behind the hermeneutical enterprise, despite the seeming merits of Gadamer's anti-methodological approach, undermine the development of an equally robust pneumatology of scriptural interpretation and spiritual discernment, a development of which homiletics stands, and has stood for decades, in tremendous need.[3] Thus, I argue that hermeneutics so named (1) is incommensurate with its own meta-critical claims, and (2) impedes the development of a strictly biblical understanding of the role of the Holy Spirit in the authoring, reading, and prayerful interpretation of scripture for proclamation. This is not to ignore or downplay in any way the sense in which the Spirit (or any member of the Trinity, for that matter) is self-effacing[4] and ultimately free, but it is to ask the naïve question of our confused generation: Is there not some point, and do we not need to discern and identify the point and set up a warning marker, at which etymology meets invocation? Is there not some sense

---

3. That Barth was attacked for, and bristled at the charge of, engaging in "pneumatic exegesis" does not concern us here, as much as the substance of the enterprise so caricatured. See Karl Barth, "Preface," *Epistle to the Philippians*, 7.

4. See Thiselton, *Hermeneutics of Doctrine*; see esp. chs. 18 and 19.

in which we must take with renewed seriousness the psalmist's resolution: "Those who choose another god multiply their sorrows; their drink offerings of blood I will not pour out or take their names upon my lips" (Ps 16:4)? Must it not finally be admitted that, if any theological enterprise invites demythologizing, it is above all hermeneutics?

In the final essay, which is, properly speaking, a discourse to preachers given on an "imagined occasion" (with apologies to Kierkegaard for the description and to Barth for the format of embedded notes that appear in the body of the text), I attempt to articulate the essential tensions at work in the task of preaching, whereby I arrive at a restatement of the Christological content of Christian preaching, and a proposed definition of preaching according to what I have called elsewhere "a penitential homiletic," where penitence is understood as synonymous with faith and homiletics is identified with upbuilding love.[5] Put another way, when Christology and pneumatology are given their due theological (and therefore asymmetrical) priority over soteriology, ecclesiology, anthropology, and ethics, it becomes clearer than ever that the limits of the rhetoric of inclusion[6] and the dialectic of inclusion/exclusion need to be recognized, that homiletical theology today may take up its proper task of preserving and proclaiming the Truth in faithfulness to the Revelation of the Truth himself and of loving with truly sanctified, spirited liberality. This task, I suggest, would be much better served by a dialectic whereby a qualitative requirement is placed upon an otherwise apparently quantitative "narrowing in," so to speak, on the wideness of God's mercy. Thus, although this discourse, with its imbedded citations and fine-print insertions (à la Barth), has not been delivered as such, it and the essays with which it appears may yet be understood as ap-

---

5. Ibid.

6. The evolution of the term "inclusion" itself is deceptive and widely misunderstood, since, at its root, "to include" does not mean to invite or welcome, but to "shut in." It is simply the opposite of "exclude," "to shut out." But this *incarcerating* sense of the term has been altogether lost in the current discussion, and deserves to be exposed as an insufficient description of the liberating work of the Spirit and the mission of God. Consider, e.g., the sense in which the ideology of inclusion has attained constitutional status in the governing documents of my own denomination, the PC(USA), which, in many quarters, interprets the Gospel in terms of liberation, but for the most part fails to recognize the self-defeating nature and the self-defeating results of its insistence on "diversity and inclusiveness" as shortcuts to the kingdom, rather than the spiritual fruits and byproducts of the Holy Spirit. See *BO*, G-4.0400; G-5.0103; G-9.0104; G-11.0103d; W-1.4003; W-3.1003; W-2.4006.

proaching a programmatic statement on the need for a narrow/broad dialectic, one that itself must be interpreted in light of the penitential dialectic I have set forth elsewhere in terms of the relation: From/To.

To repeat, however, lest a "narrow/broad" dialectic be mistaken as a matter of a "more or less" relaxed criteria, Jesus' teaching regarding the narrow gate, which forms the subject of the two sermons "included" here, makes clear that, while the two terms sound comparative and relative, the destinations toward which they lead—life and destruction, respectively—are ultimately, absolutely, infinitely qualitatively different and eternally disjoint. Mainline preaching can no longer afford to ignore this great chasm, especially where lectionary preaching, whether intentionally or not, presents us with a reduced canon that eliminates any mention of the narrow gate that leads to life and foolishly attempts to paper over this qualitative distinction.

This then leads me to the final major concern from which these essays proceed, namely, the deep, anguished conviction that "what the Spirit is saying to the churches" is to be discovered through precisely those texts that we systematically ignore. Thus, the present volume may also be understood as a prologue of sorts to *Year D* (forthcoming),[7] in which the aim is to "gather up the fragments left over" (John 6:12) after "the crowd" has finished feasting on the Word. A penitential and dialectical homiletic that aspires to faithfulness can attempt no less.

---

7. See Slemmons, "Expand the Lectionary!"

"Not Our Ways"

Diastasis *as Karl Barth's Enduring* Realdialektik *and an Exercise for Homiletical Pedagogy*

What, then, do I mean when I say that a perception of the "inner dialectic of the matter" in the actual words of the text is a necessary and prime requirement for their understanding and interpretation? It has been asserted—a Swiss reviewer has said it particularly roughly—that I mean, of course, my own "system." I know that I have laid myself open to the charge of imposing a meaning upon the text rather than extracting its meaning from it, and that my method implies this. My reply is that, if I have a system, it is limited to a recognition of what Kierkegaard called the "infinite qualitative distinction" between time and eternity, and to my regarding this as possessing negative as well as positive significance: "God is in heaven, and thou art on earth." The relation between such a God and such a man, and the relation between such a man and such a God, is for me the theme of the Bible and the essence of philosophy. Philosophers name this the KRISIS of human perception—the Prime Cause: the Bible beholds at the same cross-roads—the figure of Jesus Christ. (Karl Barth, "Preface to the Second Edition" [1921], *The Epistle to the Romans*)

Jesus said to them, "I will ask you one question; answer me, and I will tell you by what authority I do these things. Did the baptism of John come from heaven, or was it of human origin? Answer me." They argued with one another, "If we say, 'From heaven,' he will say, 'Why then did you not believe him?' But shall we say, 'Of human origin'?"—they were afraid of the crowd, for all regarded John as truly a prophet. So they answered Jesus, "We do not know." And Jesus said to them, "Neither will I tell you by what authority I am doing these things." (Mark 11:29–33)

Introduction

THIS ESSAY VENTURES A PEDAGOGICAL APPROPRIATION OF WHAT KARL Barth termed, in the preface to the second edition to his commentary on *Romans*, "a necessary and prime requirement for . . . understanding and interpretation" of "the actual words of the (biblical) text."[1] Barth's description of the "inner dialectic of the matter," however, "the matter" being that of scriptural interpretation, requires some clarification. In its original setting, the use of the term *dialectic* in the quotation which serves as the first of two epigraphs for this essay indicates a dialectic between, on the one hand, what can be known via the human enterprise of historical criticism (to which, Barth charged, most modern commentaries confined themselves, assuming that they had done the work of interpretation), and on the other hand, what can be discerned only through the revelation of Jesus Christ. Historical criticism, to which Barth offers no objections per se, is not yet interpretation. For Barth, the latter does not even begin until the temporal and the human are brought into dialectical relation with the eternal and the divine.

Dialectical is a term often used to categorize Barth's theological method as well as those of his contemporaries, Rudolf Bultmann, Emil Brunner, Friedrich Gogarten, Eduard Thurneysen, "and to a lesser extent Paul Tillich."[2] The term, however, lends itself to a certain confusion as it is often used in various senses to describe widely divergent relations. For this reason, §1 of this essay will identify the sense or senses in which this term may be applied to Barth's understanding of biblical interpretation, that is, the form(s) of dialectic which endured over the course of his dogmatic project. Toward this end, I will take stock of two attempts, by Princeton professors Daniel Migliore and Bruce McCormack, to clarify the term as Barth himself employed it. In each case, as well as in Barth scholarship generally, dialectic must be understood in its relation to analogy, the dominant school of thought regarding Barth's use of dialectic being that these two "methods" are to be taken as alternatives to one another, and further, that Barth's method took a "turn" from dialectic to analogy around 1930. We shall see, however, that both analogy and dialectic were operative throughout Barth's work. Specifically, the enduring form of dialectic, what McCormack terms the *diastasis*

1. The first epigraph to this essay is taken from Karl Barth, "The Preface to the Second Edition," *Romans*, 10. See also McCormack, *CRDT*, 11–12. McCormack's own translation rightly places qualifying quotation marks around the word "system," as the context shows it was not Barth's choice of term.

2. Busch, "Dialectical Theology," 100–20. That the term suggests the specter of Hegel, and more importantly for homiletical theology, Kierkegaard's qualitative dialectic, his attack on Hegel, and the enormous debt owed to Kierkegaard by the dialectical theologians of the twentieth century—these considerations should not be missed.

between Creator and creature, between divinity and humanity, is what I seek to uphold for homiletical pedagogy where it impinges on the issue of interpretation.

Barth's work in support of proclamation, however, continues to meet with stiff resistance in the homiletical community. §2 will engage recent objections to Barth's view of hermeneutics and his theology of preaching that have been raised within homiletical circles by David Buttrick and Ruthanna B. Hooke. In each case, I will briefly summarize the critic's concerns and venture a response from primary sources.

Finally, in §3, I will suggest a pedagogical exercise by which homiletics might aid students to identify this *diastatic* dialectic at work in Jesus' sayings in the Gospel of Mark. The dialectic we will identify, however, is not one that is confined to specific parts of the canon. Rather, by taking account of the *ultimate* diversity up front, namely, the "infinite qualitative difference" between the ways of God and the ways of human beings, such a dialectic calls into question the ultimate equivocality and cacophanous plurality of hermeneutical claims. By identifying this dialectic at work ubiquitously in Mark, I hope to further demystify this dialectic and render it more practical for homiletical interpretation.

§1. No Dearth of Dialectic: Two Welcome Clarifications

Perhaps it is best to start with a definition. *Dialectic* has been defined as "The art or practice of arriving at the truth by disclosing the contradictions in an opponent's argument and overcoming them." *Dialectics*, as a discipline, is "A method of argument or exposition that systematically weighs contradictory facts or ideas with a view to the resolution of their real or apparent contradictions." Resolution, however, is not necessarily the outcome of dialectics. Still another definition views dialectics as "The contradiction between two conflicting forces viewed as the determining factor in their continued interaction."[3] What is common to these definitions is the element of (either real or apparent) *contradiction*. Further, we note that the derivation of the term carries both dialogical-disputatious (Gk. *dialektikē*) and idiomatic-linguistic (Gk. *dialektos*) connotations. In other words, *dialectic* is not only inherently (1) aware of and open to difference and contradiction as *a priori* presuppositions,

---

3. *AHD*, 391–92. Other definitions associate the term with the philosophical and socio-materialist theories of Hegel and Marx, respectively.

not as *a posteriόri* complications, and (2) tolerant of a lack of resolution; it is also (3) potentially conversational in a sense that is hospitable to homiletics, and (4) attuned to the linguistic particulars of distinct idioms or *dialects*. This would suggest that certain of the criticisms which we will encounter (in §2) below are already anticipated and at work in the nature of dialectic itself. Meanwhile, however, we must enumerate the particular ways in which Barth employs the term *dialectic*. The first of the two clarifications to which we will attend concerns Barth's earliest dogmatic lectures.[4]

§1.1 Daniel Migliore's Synopsis of Barth's Dialectic

In his introductory essay to Karl Barth's *Göttingen Dogmatics*, Daniel Migliore is quick to note that a "dialectic understanding of revelation marks Barth's treatment of all the loci" in these seminal lectures from 1924–1925.[5] While he goes on to explain the four senses in which the term *dialectic* is used in "Karl Barth's First Lectures in Dogmatics," Migliore tips his hand by first distinguishing Barth's dialectic from that of Hegel. In contrast to Hegelian logic which resolves thesis and antithesis into a grand synthesis, the primary sense in which Barth understands dialectic pertains to "the hiddenness of God in the event of revelation."

> God's revelation is always hidden revelation, always grounded in God's free grace alone. But equally true, God's hiddenness is revealed hiddenness and is not to be identified with the inaccessibility of supposedly transcendental realities. God truly reveals Godself, yet without ceasing to be hidden, without ceasing to be the free, living Lord. God freely becomes an object for our knowledge while yet remaining indissolubly subject. In revelation God is knowable but never comprehensible.[6]

---

4. Widely considered one of Barth's clearest and earliest statements regarding his dialectical method, his lecture entitled, "The Word of God and the Task of the Ministry," delivered at Elgersburg on October 3, 1922, evinces his early recognition of the superiority of dialectic over both *mysticism* and *dogmatism*; in short, to regard him as either a "neo-orthodox" dogmatician or a "spiritualist" is equally simplistic. See Barth, *WGWM*, 183–217.

5. Migliore, "Karl Barth's First Lectures," xv–lxii, esp. xxvii–xxxiv.

6. Ibid., xxvii.

As Migliore explains the four senses of dialectic, however, this primary sense must await further clarification by way of two other forms of dialectic, placing it third in his list of four. These are: (1) the *dialectic of concepts*, (2) the *dialectic of existence*, (3) the *dialectic of revelation* (and hiddenness), and (4) *dialectic as a theological method*.

The *conceptual* dialectic recognizes that any concept can only be addressed by taking account of its opposite. Such concepts thus occur in "dialectical pairs." Revelation and hiddenness constitute but one such pair among many, including that of "necessity and contingency." Migliore observes, however, that this dialectic "is theologically inadequate since God cannot be imprisoned in any conceptual scheme. If God were subsumed within a conceptual dialectic, however sophisticated, the relationship between God and the world would be symmetrical and reversible, and the world in its contingency would be as necessary to God as God is to the world." Because "God is God," however, and not humanity's equal, such a symmetry is a theological impossibility.

The *existential dialectic* wrestles with the contradictions that are evident in human experience, or more precisely, *within* human experience. Such contradictions are not identical with God's Word, though the Word does address us "*within* these dialectics of existence." "Not the problem of inner-worldly antinomies but the far greater antinomy of God and the world is the problem on which the dogmatic theologian has to work." Both of these dialectics are of only limited use theologically until they are brought into and subsumed under the aforementioned third *dialectic*, that *of revelation and hiddenness*. In both cases, a vertical priority is established, so to speak, an asymmetry which recognizes that the dialectic of divine revelation, in Barth's words, is "not just any dialectic."

Finally, Migliore explains Barth's *dialectical method*. As Barth states the conversational character of dogmatic dialectic, which is "nothing other than genuine, open, honest, dialogue, with no confusion between me and the other, . . . between object and subject. The aim is a purification of what I think and speak about God by what God thinks and speaks." In other words, human ways and words are to conform to God's ways and words. As Migliore puts it, "the Word of God (is) to define all our concepts." But clearly God's ways are not yet our ways. "Only in heaven will we no longer need dialectical thinking."[7]

We mentioned that Barth's use of dialectic must be understood in its relation to his use of analogy. Here Migliore offers four senses in which Barth makes use of analogy. These are: (1) "negative analogies" or the "*analogia crucis*;" (2) "positive analogies in the human sphere of faith" or an early form of the *analogia fidei* which Barth only fully developed in the *Church Dogmatics*; (3) "the *analogia magnalium Dei*, 'analogy of the mighty acts of God'"; and (4) *the analogia relationis*, which did not figure in the *Göttingen Dogmatics* at all, but played "a very important role in the *Church Dogmatics*." What is important to note here is that Barth is most free with his positive analogies when treating of God's mighty acts, when drawing "an analogy between the relationship of the three forms of the Word of God and the communion of the persons of the Trinity" or when he "speaks of an analogy between God's creation of the world, the conception of the Incarnate Word by the Holy Spirit, and the resurrection of the dead." Further, "Barth affirms analogies among classical Christian doctrines." On the other hand, positive analogies between human actions and God's actions pertain exclusively to the sphere of faith, and even then, they are but analogies. Otherwise, all analogies between God and human existence take the *negative* form. "Barth speaks of human experiences of limitation and, above all, of the inescapability of death as events that may becomes negative analogies of the mystery, inaccessibility, and hiddenness of God."[8] Thus we see that Barth's use of analogy operates according to the same presupposition as his dialectic. We are left with the inescapable reminder that God's ways are *not* our ways (Isa 55:6–9; Ezek 18:24–32).

§1.2 Bruce McCormack's Corrective to von Balthasar

In his introductory essay considered above, Migliore observes that readers of the 1924–1925 *Göttingen Dogmatics* "may be surprised to discover that"—in addition to the prominence given to dialectic—"analogical thinking also flourishes."

> Contrary to the reigning model of the development of Barth's theology, it is much too simplistic to talk of the pre-*Church*

7. Ibid., xxviii–xxix.
8. Ibid., xxxii–xxxiii.

Dogmatics period as the period of dialectic that was then re-placed by the period of analogy.

Migliore is alluding to the regnant theory of Hans Urs von Balthasar who suggested that Barth's theology took a sharp method-ological turn from dialectic to analogy with his book on Anselm, *Fides quaerens intellectum* (1931).[9] Migliore refers the reader to "the fine dissertation" by Bruce McCormack,[10] which McCormack later devel-oped into a landmark study.[11] Not only did McCormack expand the scope of his research to include the span of years from 1909 to 1936, he also convincingly demonstrated the reductionistic character von Balthasar's theory.

McCormack cites the work of Ingrid Spieckermann,[12] who identi-fies "the presence of a form of analogy in Barth's 'dialectical phase,'" a dis-covery later independently confirmed by Michael Beintker.[13] Beintker, for his part, provides a helpful differentiation of four forms of dialectic at work in the second edition of Barth's *Der Römerbrief* (1922) that preceded the Göttingen lectures by two years. Following McCormack's summation of Beintker, we find a clear correspondence between two of the four forms of dialectic in question and those identified by Migliore. As these two are most easily dealt with, we will treat them first.

In the Introduction to his study, McCormack *first* mentions the "noetic" dialectical method, the *Denkform*, which Migliore mentions last. This dialectic is best exemplified by Barth's 1922 lecture, "The Word of God and the Task of the Ministry."[14] We can do no better than to al-low Barth himself to state his dialectical assertion, which not only lends structure to this lecture, but also exemplifies, to a considerable extent, the type of precise theological statement he will unfold meticulously over the course of his entire dogmatic program:

9. Urs von Balthasar, *Theology of Karl Barth*.

10. McCormack, "Scholastic of a Higher Order."

11. McCormack, *CRDT*.

12. Speickermann, *Gotteserkenntnis*.

13. McCormack, *CRDT*, 10–11. The title of Michael Beintker's book is significant: *Die Dialektik in der 'dialektischen Theologie' Karl Barths*. In addition, Migliore and McCormack both cite Beintker, "Unterricht in der christlichen Religion," in Sauter (ed.), *Verkündigung and Forschung*.

14. Barth, *WGWM*, 183–217. See n. 3 above.

> *As ministers we ought to speak of God. We are human, however,*
> *and so cannot speak of God. We ought therefore to recognize both*
> our obligation and our inability *and by that very recognition give*
> *God the glory.*[15]

Most remarkable here is that stark lack of resolution or synthesis—
between the divine and the human—which irresolution, so to speak,
will typify what McCormack will later describe as *diastasis.*

Migliore's second dialectic appears last on McCormack's list,
namely, the *dialectic of* (contradictory human) *existence* or "the dialectic
of life." So far so good. We have a one-to-one correspondence between
two of the four types of dialectic in both *Romans* II and *DGD.* But the
correspondence does not proceed quite so neatly from here.

McCormack does not explicitly mention the *dialectic of concepts.*
Why the omission? Perhaps we can account for it based on the fact that
the conceptual dialectic is so basic to the lexical sense of the term that
Barth only added this definition in his later lectures with a view to his
pedagogical task. In other words, he likely saw no need to define the
term *non-theologically* in the scathing critique of the academy that we
find in *Romans* II. But if the dialectic of concepts is *not* explicitly defined in *Romans* II, what form of dialectic identified therein by Beintker
and McCormack made way for this pedagogical sense in *DGD*?

In fact, where Migliore sees in *DGD* only one other dialectic, namely, the dialectic of revelation and hiddenness, McCormack and Beintker
see one overarching "*Realdialektik*—a dialectic in objectively real relations," that is, independent of human perception, which nevertheless
takes two forms. This is the point at which McCormack introduces the
passage that we have used as the first epigraph to the present essay. But
before we distinguish between these two forms, it will be helpful to name
their commonalities. According to McCormack's synopsis of Beintker,
the dialectic of *time and eternity* appears to be at work in *both* forms of
Realdialektik, "employed as a conceptual apparatus for bearing witness
to what is in fact a *soteriological* theme" (emphasis mine). Further, both
forms are *eschatological.* These two forms may be thus distinguished in
the following manner. The first is historically eschatological, pertaining
to the "events which occurred in AD 1–30 in the life of Christ. The sec-

---

15. Ibid., 186.

ond form focuses on the relation of an eschatologically conceived new humanity to the believer who exists in time."[16]

In his own treatment of *Romans* II, however, McCormack departs from Beintker with respect to this distinction in subtle ways. For him, the first of these two dialectics pertains to the old and the new creations, typified by Adam and Christ.[17] Here he makes use of the necessary *asymmetry*—necessitated by theology, that is—that Migliore noted was inherently lacking in a conventional dialectic of conceptual pairs. "This dialectic must be considered from God's standpoint, *sub specie aeterni.*" "There can be no equilibrium between Adam and Christ." This quasi-Hegelian dialectic is what McCormack, borrowing from Beintker, terms "supplementary." It is progressive, so to speak; it actually goes somewhere. Eternity breaks into time from God's side. Yet, because the decisive decision, if I may put it tautologically, is God's election made in eternity and not that made in time by the human subject, the resolution toward which it is moving remains in eternity, in God's "real reality" which humans do not and can not fully perceive. This is the predominant form of dialectic in *Romans* I, though traces of it remain in *Romans* II.

The second of these two dialectics, according to McCormack, is that which received the greater emphasis in *Romans* II, and that *to* which the time and eternity dialectic bears witness, namely, the dialectic of revelation and hiddenness or "veiling and unveiling." This is what McCormack sees as "a static dialectic" of "the Kierkegaardian type" (as is that of time and eternity). It is this form that Barth used "to prevent any illegitimate synthesis of God and humanity from the human side. What is in view here is a dialectic of the strictly-to-be-maintained opposition." "The 'infinite qualitative difference' between God and the world is not set aside; it is preserved."[18] The distinction between these two "real dialectics," however, would not itself remain static. By 1936, Barth would also view the dialectic of veiling and unveiling in asymmetrical terms.[19]

16. McCormack, *CRDT*, 12.

17. Ibid., 266–69.

18. Ibid., 269–70.

19. Ibid., 459–60.

At this point, we must leave those who wish to trace the subtle shifts in Barth's theological development to take up McCormack's formidable thesis on their own. Our aim is not to chart Barth's theological development. While McCormack can insist that "the riddle of how Barth's theology developed will not be solved" in terms of dialectic and analogy,[20] it is enough for us to note that his reasons for so saying are based on solid evidence that Barth employed various forms of analogy prior to *and* following the hypothetical (but by now highly suspect) "turn" to analogy and that he likewise was thoroughly engaged with various forms of dialectic throughout his dogmatic program as well. McCormack does concede that there was a certain shift *in emphasis* away from the dialectical *method*, but he insists that von Balthasar portrayed this shift as a radical, qualitative break. This method, however, is not the dialectic we have in view.[21] Rather, our purpose is to consider the *Realdialektik* which endured throughout Barth's career, that which was not only *not* abandoned with the increased emphasis on the *analogia fidei* and the *analogia relationis*, but *could not* be abandoned precisely due to the dialectical nature of these doctrines.[22] The distinctions McCormack makes between these two forms of *Realdialektik* pertain primarily to *Romans* II. Despite Barth's own admission that the second edition of his commentary was given to "powerful one-sidedness," McCormack rightly observes: "even in his most repentant moments, Barth never said that the diastasis motif which governed *Romans* II was wrong; it was rather—like all heresies worth their salt—a half-truth." In light of this self-critique, we might even say, while it is variously described in terms of hiddenness and revelation, judgment and grace, the Creator and the creature, the divine and the human, and "wholly other" *diastasis*—the dialectic between the temporal and the eternal is one that comes up again and again in Barth's larger output, to the extent that even the two (supplementary and complementary) sub-forms of dialectic identified

---

20. Ibid., 14. Rather, McCormack identifies, among other things, a "shift from a process eschatology to a consistent (i.e. radically futurist) eschatology"; 202.

21. Ibid., 1–20; esp. 12–13, 16.

22. "'Dialectical method' *could* have been abandoned altogether—in truth, it was not, but it could have been—without in the least requiring the abandonment of the vastly more important *Realdialektik*. The great weakness of the von Balthasarian formula is that it conceals from view the extent to which Karl Barth remained—even in the *Church Dogmatics*!—a *dialectical theologian*." McCormack, *CRDT*, 18, 278–79.

by McCormack in *Romans* II seem to be dialectically related. Most significant for our purposes, however, is that McCormack is able, at only the mid-point of his dense thesis, to resolve

> to demonstrate throughout the remainder of this book, (that) Barth never turned away from the starting-point which was embodied in the diastasis motif. The diastasis certainly had to be reformulated—in terms other than those provided by a consistent eschatology. But the "wholly otherness" of God would remain a permanent feature of Barth's thought. The thesis to be argued here is that the gains made in *Romans* II are everywhere presupposed throughout the *Church Dogmatics*; that the continuity in theological perspective between these two great works so greatly outweighs the discontinuity that those who wish to read the dogmatics without the benefit of the lens provided by *Romans* II will understand everything in the wrong light.[23]

As bold as this claim may seem with regard to Barth studies, when we consider that the pivotal work in question was a manifesto (of sorts) of dialectical scriptural interpretation and that Barth's dogmatic lectures were at every point undertaken to support the task of proclamation, it nevertheless seems fair to say that it is not simply Barth's dogmatics which are at risk of being read in the wrong light by those without the proper lenses, but scripture itself.

§2. Two Contemporary Critiques

Having identified the enduring dialectic in Barth's works as the *diastasis*, the "infinite qualitative difference" between the divine and the human, the eternal and the temporal, revelation and hiddenness, we will now turn to consider two objections that have been raised to Barth from the homiletical academy. The challenges to be considered here are those issued by David Buttrick and Ruthanna B. Hooke. Following a summary of each argument, I will venture a reply from a standpoint that keeps the *diastasis* in view.

§2.1 David Buttrick

In his Foreword to Karl Barth's *Homiletics*, David Buttrick outlined *in nuce* several aspects of Barth's theology of preaching that he found

23. McCormack, *CRDT*, 244.

"peculiar."[24] These aspects are, broadly speaking: (1) Barth's denial of a "'point of contact,' some predisposition in the self that will align with the gospel"; (2) his "attack on 'relevance'"; and (3) his notorious biblicism. Three years later, Buttrick elaborated on this list of features in his book, *A Captive Voice*,[25] though the list itself had not changed. Rather, these same features of Barth's homiletical theory repeatedly serve as the lightning rod for Buttrick's criticism. Buttrick voices his suspicion that certain "good things—Bible, church and Christian identity in the world . . . may have turned against us."[26] His thesis unfolds in four chapters. One chapter each is dedicated to these three subjects (the Bible, the church, and culture), followed by a fourth chapter on method and an "Afterword."

Chapter 1 seeks to liberate preaching from its captivity to the Bible, or more precisely, to biblicism. Buttrick sees the movement to biblical theology begun with Barth as having "turned against us" in the form of fundamentalism.[27] Fundamentalism takes Barth's Word of God theology to such an extreme that it confuses the Bible with the gospel,[28] while Barth himself even "personified scripture."[29] Further, by denying

---

24. Barth, *Homiletics*, 7–11, esp. 8–9.

25. Buttrick, *Captive Voice*. For a more recent critical, but appreciative view of Barth's homiletical contribution, see Willimon, *Conversations with Barth on Preaching*, ably reviewed (February 1, 2007) by Ingalls, "Review of *Conversations with Barth*."

26. Buttrick, *Captive Voice*, 1.

27. Ibid., 5.

28. "Christian theology has seldom equated the entire Bible—every verse, every phrase—with the gospel message. Nor has Christian theology heretofore personified the entire Bible without reservation as a passionate, pursuing Word of God. As a result of an enlarging biblical conservatism, we are hearing more and more apologetic sermons trying to justify unlikely passages as being, nevertheless, the Word of God. . . . Is the whole Bible a book that must be preached simply because it is the Bible and somebody has labeled it the Word of God?" Ibid., 11. Neither does it appear Buttrick has modified his views on Barth much in the years since the publication of *A Captive Voice*. In an (undated, but evidently post-2002) interview with Timothy Merrill of Homiletics Online, he describes the modernist-fundamentalist tension in twentieth-century homiletics as lying between Fosdickian liberalism and Barthian biblicism, making no distinction between Barth and fundamentalism, and characterizing any possible convergence between Barthian homiletics as modern liberalism as a "desperate concern" on the part of "white congregations . . . trying to hold their social position"; http://www.homileticsonline.com/subscriber/interviews/buttrick.asp.

29. Buttrick, *Captive Voice*, 7. Buttrick cites Barth's early essay to which we have twice referred: "The Word of God and the Task of the Ministry," in Karl Barth, *WGWM*, 183–217.

general or natural revelation and any possibility of arguing from experience and by stating the case for the Bible so strongly,

> Barth in some ways all but destroyed preaching in the name of the Bible. He threw out sermon introductions because they might imply some sort of "point of contact," some natural affinity for the gospel in the human sphere; and he lopped off conclusions because they might express works-righteousness. Above all, he denied social relevance: "The Preacher," he wrote, "must preach the Bible and *nothing* else."[30]

The result of this, in Buttrick's view, is that "preaching and the Bible have been wrapped up in a kind of incestuous relationship," to the extent that preaching is not allowed to address public, social, and political issues.[31] According to Buttrick, the "true hermeneutic of scripture is ultimately *social*."[32] In fact, he attributes the problems with biblicism to its very verticality. After recalling an embarrassing lecture, in which he heard an unnamed speaker consider the ways in which the baby-bashing text of Ps 137:9 might be handled homiletically—a clear case of confusing the Bible with the gospel, Buttrick observes,

> Part of the problem may have to do with the vertical notion of biblical authority. 'But how can we credit any sovereign biblical authority model in view of a God who is known in the outright helpless stupidity of the cross? . . . The biblical theology movement is a strange legacy. We have gained much from a golden age of historical-critical biblical scholarship. But maybe, just maybe, we have lost our homiletical souls—prophetic silence, past-tense faith, and an enlarging tension between the Bible and the good news of the gospel message.[33]

Historical criticism has yielded positive results, but Barth's rediscovery of the Bible has apparently not. Where Buttrick insists on the urgency of addressing hermeneutical issues, he portrays Barth's position as thoughtlessly dismissive and unsympathetic. "Hermeneutic questions are urgent. They cannot be dismissed as irrelevant by dogmatic Barthianism."[34] For Buttrick, hermeneutics is an essentially socio-anthropological and political concern.

30. Buttrick, *Captive Voice*, 8.
31. Ibid., 9.
32. Ibid., 14.
33. Ibid., 11–12.
34. Ibid., 14.

We see this socio-ethical emphasis in his treatment of Barth's rejection of natural theology as well.

> The phrase "ultimate concern" echoes truth; human beings try to grasp the meaning of their lives in relation to God—and often without the benefit of scripture. / But, as all good religions insist, we know God through symbols, often through symbols encountered ritually. As Christians we know God through the living symbol, Jesus Christ. He is the model of our lives, as well as source of our faith, hope, and love. The idea of Jesus Christ as a disclosure model for God was built into most of us ritually long before we were able to read our Bibles.[35]

Buttrick apparently understands the pre-literate child's oral instruction and ritual imitation—he is, after all, the child of a famous preacher—as "natural revelation," quite independent of the Bible. If, on the other hand, this ritual imparting of Jesus Christ as an "idea of . . . a disclosure model" is a reference to the sacrament of baptism, Buttrick makes no claim here for any qualitative distinction that would set Christian baptism apart from initiation into any other "religion," a category under which he subsumes not only the sacrament, but the gospel itself.

In chapter 2, Buttrick considers the ways in which preaching has been held captive by the church. Ironically, the chapter begins by turning to scripture to demonstrate "the Bible's sure confidence in the Word preached."[36] Buttrick notes that the resurrection appearances in which the disciples were commissioned to preach depict preaching as an activity that is to take place both outside and inside the church. Further, these passages are thoroughly apocalyptic, all of which indicates that preaching is not to be confined to the church. Rather, "preaching is God's word, *not our word.*"[37] The Reformers, we are reminded, set "the voice of preaching up *over* the church."[38] "The church is subservient to the preached Word of God." But more recently, the congregation has unseated preaching. Liturgical reform has tended to view preaching as

---

35. Ibid., 20. We may wonder what specifically would figure on Buttrick's short list of "good religions," but we can be sure of at least one that will not be excluded; see 106.

36. Ibid., 36.

37. Ibid., 38; emphasis mine.

38. Ibid., 38–43.

more and more a part of the liturgy, but not in any sense above it. Here, Buttrick affirms Barth's emphasis on the sacraments as an essential part of proclamation, and though he does not acknowledge it, Barth would agree with his recognition of the precedence of the Word over the sacraments.[39]

But more than liturgy has overthrown the pulpit. The consumer-driven approach to ministry has turned preachers into "enablers." The market demand for spiritual goods and services now sets the agenda. Neither the church growth expert Lyle Schaller, nor a stereotyped Duke School sectarianism is a fit substitute for evangelism. Buttrick concludes, "some of the blame must be handed over to Karl Barth. Barth had little interest in any wisdom the world might offer; he had no real wish to engage the world in conversation. His focus was on revelation and faith alone."[40] Buttrick definitely sees a place for apologetics, which Barth considered largely self-defeating, since God alone is proof of God's existence, and further, God prohibits the manufacture of the very images on the basis of which apologetics makes its appeals.[41]

Though he does not mention Barth again in this chapter on the church, we should note certain of Buttrick's own peculiarities with which the chapter concludes. On the one hand, Buttrick wants to reclaim the "apocalyptic urgency" of the preaching of Jesus, who proclaimed that the kingdom of God is at hand. "Once more let us announce the coming of God's new order." But somehow, Buttrick perceives that this new order will emerge horizontally. Again, he dismisses theology oriented toward the vertical.

> Have you noticed there seems to be a pendulum swing in the history of preaching? There are times when the gospel seems to be defined by *vertical analogy*: a human world below and a God world above. In such times, the pulpit tends to elevate Christ himself . . . But in other eras *vertical analogies* have crumbled. They are in-between periods, often gripped by a sense of apocalyptic urgency, and they seem to understand the world horizontally. In such periods, the pulpit stands once more with Christ to

39. Ibid., 44; see also Barth, *CD* 1/1:70–71. Barth insists that preaching and the sacraments are inseparable, but "the sacrament (exists) for the sake of preaching, not *vice versa.*"

40. Buttrick, *Captive Voice*, 48–49.

41. Barth, *Homiletics*, 47.

proclaim the coming of what Jesus called the *basileou to theou*, "kingdom of God."[42]

In chapter 3, Buttrick addresses the role of the church in relation to the culture. When confronting the culture, the first step is the translation of the faith into the language of the culture, but explanation of the faith must soon follow, and explanation requires metaphor, simile, and analogy.[43] Buttrick upholds Barth as the paradigm of the church's withdrawal from collapsing alliances with the culture.[44] But he approvingly quotes Barth's observation that we live "between the times."[45] For Buttrick, however, this means we live in times of change, between epochs of history, not between the old age and the new age, not as Barth portrayed it in *Romans* I, in the dialectic between Adam and Christ.[46]

> So how do we preach? What is the task of homiletics now? We must still separate Christianity from an earlier synthesis. We must separate ourselves from a cultural formulation now in disarray. To do so, the pulpit must be culturally critical. Instead of Barth's turn from culture in the name of an imperious biblicism, we must be willing to take on cultural assumptions that are no longer viable: our blind faith in technological progress, our reliance on the power of death—Is the Pentagon our national monument?—the all-pervasive "triumph of the therapeutic," and other cultural idols. . . . But, here's the catch, we must take on ourselves as well. We must speak contrapuntally against an earlier synthetic Christianity that was grounded in rationalism and pietism and, yes, historicism. To borrow a term

42. Buttrick, *Captive Voice*, 49–50. While it is my intention to postpone my rejoinder until later, what is not at all clear at this point is precisely how apocalyptic acquires this horizontal trajectory, which seems incommensurate with Buttrick's subsequent observations that (1) we suffer from total depravity, and (2) God's Word "is *not* human wisdom, a technology, or a therapeutic insight." See ibid., 50–52.

43. Ibid., 56–61.

44. Ibid., 61–63.

45. Ibid., 71–72.

46. Ibid., 63–71. In a slapdash "sketch of cultural phases"—which he himself admits will "be enough to offend any competent historian"—Buttrick attempts to deconstruct "any attempt to live in a vertical stasis forever, enjoying vertical pieties under an elaborately woven sacred canopy" as "a form of cultural idolatry." Though the phrase "vertical stasis" and what McCormack terms *diastasis* are not identical, they do suggest a similar orientation; nevertheless, it is hard to imagine that the falsely pious triumphalism Buttrick aims to deconstruct bears any resemblance to Barth's assertion that theology is done beneath the "sword of Damocles." Barth, *DGD*, 5 and 61.

from Robert Jensen, we must be a "religion against itself." For such a task, Barth's radical dialectical theology can be useful. Between the ages, preaching must still be committed to cultural disengagement.

Yet, must we not be as much concerned with what might be termed reengagement? Like it or not, we are moving toward a new evangelical enterprise. Somehow, Christian faith must seed itself in countercultural movements that will someday come together to form a new social mind. Once more we are called on to translate ourselves into the thought forms and images of a forming new age.[47]

Buttrick recalls the influence of H. Richard Niebuhr's *Christ and Culture* and the paradigms for their relation, though, significantly, he mentions only four of the five, omitting "Christ the Transformer of Culture."[48] He then suggests new categories are needed to address these issues. Buttrick is certain of one thing, however: "We can no longer live in the world chanting Karl Barth's emphatic '*Nein.*'"[49] Nevertheless, he ends the chapter confessing he has no satisfactory answer to the questions: "How can we preserve the integrity of our Christian faith against the world? Where is the essence of the Christianity we are supposed to preserve?" Instead, Buttrick simply chants his own emphatic *Nein!* to Barth, who serves as his caricature of the irrelevant sectarian.[50]

> There is no pure gospel; no, not even in the Bible! To be blunt, the Christian scriptures are both sexist and anti-Semitic. Faith is ever an admixture with cultural notions. Perhaps all we can do is to preach at the point of our conversion from the mind of the age, and leave the rest to the working of the Holy Spirit.[51]

Buttrick's protest is passionately muddled. He admits no possibility that Barth's consideration of these questions might yield important affirmations regarding the need for purity of doctrine or correctives to the "mind of the age" that would not simply replace this with a new "so-

---

47. Buttrick, *Captive Voice*, 72–74.

48. Niebuhr, *Christ and Culture*, esp. 190–229.

49. Buttrick, *Captive Voice*, 74.

50. Buttrick says nothing of the political emphasis in Barth's early career. Further, he sees Barth's political move in authoring the Barmen Declaration as offset by the "biblical isolation" from public affairs which characterized his sermons from the period; ibid., 8.

51. Ibid., 75.

cial mind," or a sociological hermeneutic that judges and subordinates the authority of scripture.

Not surprisingly, by the time we reach chapter 4, Barth does not figure in Buttrick's methodological proposal at all. The chapter is, in short, a rehash of Buttrick's massive, award-winning *Homiletic: Moves and Structures*.[52] The challenge for homiletical method is how to present the gospel to "an emerging, quite different human consciousness."[53] Structural attention to both narrative and rhetorical logic must be reclaimed. "Moves" must replace propositional points. Attention to form is required in order to influence the hearer's "hermeneutical response."[54] Sermons must be presented from various points-of-view. One of the few indirect references to Barth is again negative. Biblical preaching, we are told, is a "myth," a "shibboleth." "Let us admit the truth: In a way, none of us preach directly from the Bible. Not really. Perhaps the whole notion of biblical preaching is a popular fallacy." The debates between Barth and Bultmann "were silly because every preacher automatically demythologizes."[55] As if to underscore this capitulation with a great flourish, Buttrick brings the chapter to a close with a proposal for preaching on the Parable of the Rich Man and Lazarus (Luke 16:19–31). I will not summarize it here, except to highlight Buttrick's first move, which is to insist on the necessity for an introduction. "Why would we want such an Introduction?" The answer comes with breathtaking presumption: "Because we must get rid of any tendency to read any literal references to an afterlife in the parable."[56]

Buttrick adds a note explaining his hermeneutical strategy for preaching parables. The idea is to allow "the parable to unfold in consciousness, episode by episode, doing what it is *designed* to do." "No didactic points are made. Instead, you let *the structural movement* of the parable do its intended work." Buttrick himself correlates his method with Fred Craddock's notion of "overhearing the gospel."[57]

52. Buttrick, *Homiletic*.

53. Buttrick, *Captive Voice*, 80.

54. Ibid., 87–88.

55. Ibid., 89–90.

56. Ibid., 95.

57. Ibid., 98; emphasis mine. See Craddock, *Overhearing the Gospel*. I have elsewhere argued at length that Craddock's Beecher lectures, while seeking to support his method of indirect communication, represent a colossal failure to take account of

In Buttrick's "Afterword," Barth appears again as the symbol of irrelevant biblicism.[58] The way forward will require the church to turn with renewed attention to evangelism with rhetorical skill and an apologetic thrust,[59] to preaching the kingdom of God as the new social reality,[60] and to theology done with hermeneutical sensitivity to the culture. With respect to this final point, Bultmann and Ricoeur are commended.[61] Barth's theology has been chastened into silence.

§2.2 A Response to Buttrick

Not all of Buttrick's specific criticisms warrant a response, as they all derive from the three primary objections enumerated in his Foreword to Barth's *Homiletics*. Here we will consider in turn Buttrick's case against: (1) Barth's denial of a *point of contact*, (2) the question of relevance, and (3) Barth's biblicism.

Buttrick reminds the reader repeatedly that God's wisdom is not human wisdom and on at least one occasion he affirms the doctrine of total depravity. Neither does he hide his suspicion of pietism in the least. Nevertheless, he does not seem to consider the full implications of total depravity or the "wholly otherness" of God's Word on the homiletical claim for a point of contact. Neither does he ever manage to bring these implications to bear on the question of scriptural interpretation. We recall that while Barth repeatedly describes *diastasis* in terms of Ecclesiastes 5:2 ("God is in heaven, and thou art on earth"), Buttrick explicitly disdains any vertical orientation throughout his proposal. One could hardly contrive a better example of the need for *diastasis* as the primary presupposition for interpretation than Buttrick's sermon in which he denies, with his anti-Barthian insistence on an introduction, the very "great chasm" that separates heaven and hell (Luke 16:19–31). Total depravity provides the rationale for preaching a social vision, as though the apocalyptic kingdom of God is only ever going to arrive from

---

(1) Kierkegaard's qualitative dialectic whereby esthetics and humanistic ethics are radically distinguished from faith, and the genius from the apostle; as well as (2) Kierkegaard's own rhetorical directness in his homiletical discourses (read "lay sermons"). See Slemmons, "Penitential Homiletic," 87–112.

58. Buttrick, *Captive Voice*, 102–5.

59. Ibid., 105–8.

60. Ibid., 108–10.

61. Ibid., 110–12.

next door. What is lacking here is an appreciation of the miraculous and gracious nature of the "specific revelation" that alone is able to cross the great chasm, and cross it specifically in terms of vertical *dialectic!* Buttrick is so worried about the possibility of any such a relation being understood *analogically,*[62] that he will not consider *any* verticality, not even that dialectical relation of *diastasis* which posits the (infinite qualitative) *difference* between God's ways and human ways—a difference Buttrick himself tentatively affirms (quantitatively, I suspect), though with considerable inconsistency. Not once does he address the other reasons Barth gave for his prohibition of introductions, namely, that (1) "worship itself is the introduction to the sermon"; (2) most introductions actually *distract* the listener from the Word of God; and (3) the subject of the sermon is *not* the present age or the wicked world and its ways.[63] Most disturbing, however, is the sense that for Buttrick there is little else at stake in recognizing the *diastasis* but the use of introductions. He simply throws in his lot with Schleiermacher and goes the way of old school liberalism, instructing preachers to deny the threat of hell. Introductions will see to that.

Barth's intention regarding the question of *relevance* is also misstated. In their original context, Barth's statements are simply made in the service of a higher aim. The "aim," Buttrick fails to note, is still in the *direction* of relevance, only *higher.* "All honor to relevance, but pastors should be good marksmen who aim their guns beyond the hill of relevance."[64] Preachers are to take for granted that the Word of God is *always* relevant.[65] Here again the critique is double-minded, but without the benefit of paradox or dialectical discernment. On the one hand, Buttrick rightly criticizes the church for having overthrown the pulpit and replaced it with a psycho-therapeutic model of ministry that caters to the spiritual consumer. On the other hand, he would replace this model with one that takes as its theme the pertinent socio-political issues of the day. In other words, the individual psychological subject is ejected from the driver's seat only to have a liberal social agenda

---

62. Ibid., 49–50.

63. Barth, *Homiletics*, 121–25.

64. Ibid., 119.

65. Ibid., 128. "A sermon can often be more relevant when it does not seem to be relevant at all."

crammed in its place.[66] While Buttrick designates this new societal vision "eschatological," he does not ask: *whence shall this kingdom come?* He understands the epistemological question in strictly anthropological terms, that is, in terms of "how people think,"[67] not dialectically or theologically in terms of how sinful human beings can know *anything* with any assurance in a world in which, as he admits, "there are no earthly ultimates, only ambiguities."[68] No thought is spared for the something higher at which Barth might be aiming, "the standard by which Church proclamation is to be measured."[69]

In Barth's treatment of "the problem of dogmatics," he does indeed state the matter quite strongly, but with good reason. "Church proclamation is not an undertaking which can come under any other criteria than God's Word in respect of its content." "The choice of other criteria in place of God's Word betrays itself already as an act involving *abandonment of the Church's ground*, of its *recollection* and *expectation* and to that extent of its *faith*, by the very fact that it is a choice, an act of human perplexity and prudence, instead of an act of acknowledgment of God's prevenient goodness." Any other criteria that are "put alongside the one standard"

> are to be rejected as *irrelevant* and *injurious because* they cannot serve vicariously as surrogates, *because* all vicariate is fundamentally impossible here. Philosophy, ethics, politics and anything else that might be suggested here may all have their own dignity and justification *in their own spheres* but *they are the philosophy, ethics, and politics of sinful and lost man* whose word, however profound and true it may be, *cannot be recognised as judge over the Word* which is addressed *in the name of God* to these sinful and lost men, as judge, therefore, over Church proclamation.[70]

---

66. In this respect, Buttrick's proposal represents the state of homiletics as it has, in recent years, tried to graduate beyond the esthetic preoccupations of the New Homiletic only to become thoroughly entrenched in what Kierkegaard called the ethical sphere. But on the need to preserve the individual-communal dialectic in preaching, see Slemmons, "Penitential Homiletic," 113–82, 353–54.

67. Buttrick, *Captive Voice*, 31, 65.

68. Ibid., 50.

69. Barth, *CD* 1/1:255.

70. (Ibid., 255–56; emphasis mine.

Certainly, one might well ask of Barth what penultimate criteria, if any, God's Word authorizes, but Buttrick is quite wrong to suggest that Barth had no real wish to engage the world in such conversation,[71] as Busch's biography, McCormack's thesis, the Barmen Declaration, Barth's own sermons to prison inmates, his extensive writings on Christian ethics, or a cursory glance at the index of names in the *CD*, will attest. It is equally wrong to contend that "talk of the kingdom of God to twentieth-century neo-orthodoxy is a form of heresy," as though homiletics had the option of preaching a "social vision" that does not also involve a "personal relationship with Jesus, whatever such a phrase may mean," or a kingdom with no sovereign.[72] In both cases, Barth simply insisted on putting first things first, and he did this by refusing at every point to compromise God's "wholly otherness." Though Buttrick rightly objects that the church has diminished preaching in the name of liturgical, pragmatic, and therapeutic aims, the solution is *not* to reduce Christ Jesus from Sovereign to "living symbol," or worse yet, a mere socialist. It is, rather, to respect the authority of the Word of God as God's self-revelation, that which human beings independent of God, no matter how large the group or the group consensus, are helpless to attain.

Closely related to Buttrick's socio-ethical program is his complaint against Barth's biblicism and his apparent disregard for "urgent" hermeneutical questions. In fact, however, Barth's answer to the charge of biblicism in the Preface to *Romans* II is quite modest, and scarcely seems to warrant the shrill denunciation it receives from Buttrick.

> I have, moreover, no desire to conceal the fact that my "Biblicist" method—which means in the end no more than "consider well"—is applicable also to the study of Lao-Tse and of Goethe. Nor can I deny that I should find considerable difficulty in applying the method to certain of the books contained in the Bible itself. When I am named "Biblicist," all that can rightly be proved against me is that I am prejudiced in supposing the Bible to be a good book, and that I hold it to be profitable for men to take its conceptions at least as seriously as they take their own.[73]

One finds very little to object to here, unless, of course, one does not appreciate being told to "consider well." Admittedly, Barth was soft-

71. Buttrick, *Captive Voice*, 48.
72. Ibid., 109–10.
73. Barth, *Romans*, 12.

pedaling at this point. By 1925, however, he claimed the Bible itself as his authorization for his biblicist orientation, since the Bible proves itself to human experience.

> Biblicism, a biblical attitude, comes from the Bible itself. Read in the Bible so long that you have it, that with the help of the Old and New Testament texts you become so used to it as a rule of thought like any other. In this way, with this formal determination, we think and speak when we speak about revelation. Everything else will follow if we grasp this rule of thought, simply grasp it, without enthusiasm, experiences, or surprises.[74]

Elsewhere, Barth addresses the hermeneutical question directly, not dismissively, but so as once again to put first things first. Again, scripture continues to be self-vindicating.[75] This rationale requires not that we *personalize* scripture, as Buttrick has charged, but that we distinguish the Bible as witness from the One to whom it witnesses.[76] Barth does not deny, rather, he adamantly *affirms* the humanity of scripture, but "when we do take the humanity of the Bible quite seriously, we must also take quite definitely the fact that as a human word it does say something specific, that as a human word it points from itself, that as a word it points towards a fact, an object."[77] Barth demands: Is it ethical and loving to notice that a human being is speaking to you without paying the least attention to what it is he is saying?

> How much wrong is being continually perpetrated, how much intolerable obstruction of human relationships, how much isolation and impoverishment forced upon individuals has its only basis in the fact that we do not take seriously a claim which in itself is as clear as the day, the claim which arises whenever one person addresses a word to another.[78]

As clear as this is, Barth argues, a general anthropology or a general hermeneutics of human language can claim no success in giving the

---

74. Barth, *DGD*, 290.

75. Barth, *CD* 1/2:462. "The basic statement of this doctrine, the statement that the Bible is the witness of divine revelation, is itself based simply on the fact that the Bible has in fact answered our question about the revelation of God, bringing before us the lordship of the triune God."

76. Ibid., 463.

77. Ibid., 464.

78. Ibid., 465.

point "general recognition" and thereby improving the situation. The reason for this is that a "general hermeneutics" should actually derive its interpretive principles from the Bible and not the other way around. What is important to note here is that by "general hermeneutics" Barth does *not* mean something higher, so to speak, under which "biblical hermeneutics" is a specialization. Neither does he intend to exalt the human words of the Bible over human language generally. Nevertheless, the Bible, which "cannot be read unbiblically," provides the test case for *all* interpretation.

> It is not at all that the word of man in the Bible has an abnormal significance and function. We see from the Bible what its normal significance and function is. It is from the word of man in the Bible that we must learn what has to be learned concerning the word of man in general. This is not generally recognized. It is more usual blindly to apply to the Bible false ideas taken from some other source concerning the significance and function of the human word. But this must not confuse us into thinking that the very opposite way is the right one. *There is no such thing as a special biblical hermeneutics.* But we have to learn that hermeneutics which is alone and generally valid by means of the Bible as the witness of revelation. We therefore arrive at the suggested rule, not from a general anthropology, but from the Bible, and obviously, as the rule which is alone and generally valid, we must apply it first to the Bible.[79]

In other words, the Word of God written will always be expressed in human words, but because the Word *of God* accompanies these human words, the Bible provides the prototype for all interpretation.

In summary, for Buttrick's criticism to be convincing, it would first have to address the dialectic by which God's Word can and does accompany the human words of the Bible without collapsing the one into the other: "my thoughts are not your thoughts!" (Isa 55:8) This, in my view, would clear up most, if not all, of the points he raises. Second, compelling evidence would need to be presented for Buttrick's decidedly negative characterization of Barth's view of biblical authority, as well as a theologically sound argument for replacing it with a "general hermeneutic" or some other socio-anthropological criteria. To make the case that Barth, in fundamentalist fashion, confuses the Bible with

---

79. Ibid., 466; emphasis mine.

the gospel, and to substantiate the claim that the social reality of the eschatological kingdom is *the* "true hermeneutic," requires a demonstrable understanding of the function and purpose of the *canon*, and some sense of the reality of the Holy Spirit at work in the process of interpretation, to say nothing of a cogent articulation of *how* gospel differs from law and other genres of the Word. While these features are not in evidence in *A Captive Voice*, it is its outright denial of the diastatic dialectic that has occasioned the present rejoinder, while in the latter case, namely, with regard to the false charge of fundamentalism and the attempt to subordinate biblical authority to a socially construed horizontal hermeneutics, we plainly see the distorted results of hermeneutical "urgency" divorced from a sound and guiding doctrine of the Holy Spirit.

Apart from featuring in a handful of citations from Calvin and Luther, the Holy Spirit is portrayed as more common than holy;[80] a "God of the gaps."[81] Otherwise, the Spirit comes to mind whenever the author's thought turns to liberalism, social action, and inter-religious dialogue: though long since discredited, the time for theological liberalism has come again, if for no other reason than it has waited in the wings long enough;[82] the Spirit of God empowers civil rights leaders, such as Martin Luther King Jr., to speak the truth with "a prophetic voice, a liberation voice" to which the "compulsive biblicism" of Karl Barth bears no resemblance;[83] the Holy Spirit would have us learn from our "religious friends" of other religions (Islam alone is mentioned specifically), which "we can no longer assume . . . are the enemy because they don't clutch the same Bible as we do."[84] Such is the impoverished and distorted understanding of the work of the Holy Spirit in preaching, an understanding that can only arise where the "infinite qualitative difference" is conveniently dismissed by the grandiose claims of herme-

---

80. "Surely preaching must change and become the articulation of our common faith, a speaking from the Spirit we all possess." Buttrick, *Captive Voice*, 2; but on the age-old and largely forgotten distinction between the holy and the common, see Lev 10:10–11; Ezek 22:26 and 44:23.

81. Buttrick, *Captive Voice*, 75.

82. Ibid., 50.

83. Ibid., 104.

84. Ibid., 106.

neutics and the gaping jaws of Hades are conveniently obliterated with handy sermon introductions.

To summarize this rejoinder to *A Captive Voice: The Liberation of Preaching*, preaching is not captive to the Bible or the church; on the contrary, its power is quenched where the agency and the authority of the Holy Spirit is quenched (1 Thess 5:19), where the Spirit is grieved (Eph 4:30), where the "wholly otherness" of God, and of the Scriptures themselves, is replaced with humanly constructed socio-political programs masquerading as the "kingdom of God."

§2.3 Ruthanna B. Hooke

The second challenge to Barth's homiletics concerns his views on sermon delivery. Ruthanna B. Hooke advocates teaching homiletics courses that focus on performance considerations and she offers her insights based the experience of teaching a course at Yale entitled "Performance of Texts."[85] The course involves an "exegetical analysis to explore the meaning of the text in question, and the crafting of a performance of the text." The second of these two steps provides the rationale for the course, which appropriates the "tools and practices used by actors" for preaching. Decisive for the preacher's ability to "make present the truth of the biblical text" is the presence of the preacher herself. Hooke's proposal employs an exercise designed for acting classes that requires that the student actor say, "I am here in this room with all of you," and do so in a way that embodies the truth of the phrase with the actor's most convincing presence.[86]

Hooke anticipates at the outset that the performance enterprise will find its harshest critic in Karl Barth, primarily with respect to his doctrine of revelation and his Neo-Kantian epistemology, both of which inform his characteristic insistence on the preacher's transparency. She cites two passages, one from *CD* 1/2, in which Barth states that the Word of God "must be a selfless human word" that will not be uttered "in a spirit of self-assertion,"[87] and the other from Barth's Bonn lectures

---

85. Hooke, "'I Am Here in this Room . . .'", 13–21. For other homiletical proposals that draw on the dramatic arts, see Childers, *Performing the Word*, and Childers and Schmidt, *Performance in Preaching*.

86. Hooke, "'I Am Here in this Room . . .'", 13.

87. Barth, *CD* 1/2:764.

(1932–1933), in which he claims that the sermon should be "like the involuntary lip movements of one who is reading with great care, attention, and surprise, more following the letters than reading in the usual sense, all eyes, totally claimed, aware that '*I* have not written the text.'"[88] Hooke clearly understands Barth's aim to be "to curb possible abuses of power by the preacher." She notes his "stern admonitions" to humility, selflessness, and obedience. "Barth attempts to separate the power of preaching from the power of the preacher, so that the power of revelation might rest with God and would not accrue to the human medium through which that revelation comes."[89]

Hooke raises two objections to Barth's theology of preaching. The first objection concerns the doctrine of revelation itself and Barth's insistence on the "self-effacement" of the preacher. In her view, Barth diminishes the humanity of the preacher and robs revelation of God's commitment to respecting the historical, contextual, "embodied" particularities of human experience. Revelation, we are reminded, does not come to us in a disembodied voice from heaven.

> Rather, God's revelation, God's Word comes to us and makes sense to us in the midst of our lives, our struggles, our joys and sorrows, our relationships and our communities. . . . That God always reveals Godself to humanity in the midst of its historical, embodied existence is evident in God's paradigmatic event of self-revelation, the incarnation, life, death and resurrection of Jesus Christ. In Jesus Christ, God reveals Godself not by bypassing humanity but by inhabiting humanity, the particular historical and embodied humanity of Jesus Christ. . . . Even if it is true, as Barth claims, that God alone overcomes our inability to know God, . . . the doctrine of the Incarnation suggests what our own experience of God confirms; namely, that God reveals Godself to us not by canceling our humanity but by making us active partners with God in revelation.[90]

Hooke's second objection concerns the power of the preacher. She contends that Barth's notion of transparency, intended "to limit the power and influence of the preacher so that God's revelation may

---

88. Barth, *Homiletics*, 76. Hooke does not include the final clause. I have restored it here, however, as it carries the emphasis which I think Barth intended.

89. Hooke, "'I Am Here in this Room . . .'", 15.

90. Ibid., 16.

be unhindered by human 'self-assertion,'" backfires on him in such a way as to actually "collapse the human presence of the preacher into God's presence, the preacher's voice into God's voice." "The preacher who speaks only for God, and not from her own humanity, inescapably usurps divine power in the event of preaching."[91]

Having cleared the way for her proposal, Hooke explains the Yale course in further detail. Again, the doctrine of revelation presupposed here emphasizes the thoroughly particularistic, historical and embodied nature of God's self-disclosure, especially in the Incarnation of Jesus Christ. It is in this light that the course encourages students "to bring their humanity into active participation in God's revelation."[92] The first step in the process is to teach "students how to be present in a room, how to be embodied humans in their speaking with others."[93] The dramatic principle that is brought to the preaching task places the preacher in "active relationship" with the text: "the truth of a text or character emerges not when the performer effaces herself before the text, as Barth urges, but when she enters into active relationship with it, when she brings her body, voice, and life experience to bear upon the text." Hooke indicates the similarities between this approach and the philosophical hermeneutics advanced by Hans-Georg Gadamer in his *Truth and Method*, one in which a "fusion of horizons" is brought about in the conversation between text and reader. The performance course, she reiterates, "essentially teaches the practice of the hermeneutical theory that Gadamer articulates."[94]

91. Ibid.

92. Ibid.

93. Ibid., 17.

94. Hooke is not the first in recent homiletical theory to draw positively upon Gadamer. Others, such as Lucy Rose, John McClure, and Richard Eslinger have taken a positive view of Gadamer's constructive importance for preaching, but the main work on Gadamerian homiletics has been done by Jeffrey Bullock, *Preaching With a Cupped Ear*, wherein the primary concern is not sermon delivery, but a philosophical understanding of the preacher's conversational interactions with the biblical text and the congregation. While his abundant pastoral sensibilities are much in evidence in his ambitious proposal, I am not as sanguine as is my friend and colleague President Bullock concerning the ability of Gadamer's theory to shore up the hermeneutical foundation that (as Bullock correctly observes) is lacking in the New Homiletic. At the risk of staking out a contrary and (biblically speaking) radical position, here I will attempt to elucidate what I consider the distorting effects of Gadamer's theory on a properly qualitative (Kierkegaardian/Barthian) dialectic in chapter 2, which effects are most clearly evident in Gadamer's reception and interpretation of the concept of contemporaneity.

Hooke upholds two of the many benefits of the Yale course. First, such performance courses teach "the importance of being present," in all the preacher's embodied particularity, which presence is, in her view, "revolutionary for the practice of preaching." Second, Hooke commends the communal nature of the performance course, particularly as it fosters a more conversational (as opposed to a monological) homiletic, one that is more open to a plurality of voices. In this respect, Hooke seeks to ally herself with the homiletical models of Lucy Rose, John McClure, and Ronald Allen.

§2.4 A Response to Hooke

Clearly Barth is a formidable theological figure who must be engaged critically. One might assume there would be available in his vast production any number of responses to Hooke's brief proposal. In fact, however, sermon performance really does amount to a lacuna in Barth's thought, relatively speaking, mainly because he thought so little of it and did so intentionally.[95] My aim here is not so much to mount a defense of Barth. Neither will I attempt to address every question raised by Hooke's essay. Rather, I will again offer those constructive suggestions that arise most clearly in the light of the *Realdialektik*, the "infinite qualitative difference" or *diastasis* that the present proposal endeavors to uphold. With this qualification in mind, I would suggest Hooke's proposal on behalf of sermon performance could be strengthened were she to consider more thoroughly and carefully the following concerns.

First, while Hooke is quite right to insist on the historical particularity of the human situation in or *into* which God's revelation speaks—the *where?*, if you will, the critical question Barth's dialectic of revelation *and hiddenness* poses is: *whence?* We need only recall that Barth's dialectical "system" as stated in the preface to *Romans* II was to be understood "as possessing negative as well as positive significance: 'God is in heaven, and thou art on earth'" (Eccl 5:2).[96] Not simple dialectics, but this peculiarly *theological* dialectic, or *diastasis*, insists that the particular human situation be brought into the vertical relation.

---

95. See Rottman's helpful essay, "Performative Language," 67–86, esp. 76–77, in which we are duly reminded of the overarching covenantal framework of our considerations of agency and performance in preaching.

96. Barth, *Romans*, 10.

Second, there is the question of the necessity of the dogmatic enterprise generally. Dogmatics is the theological discipline to which the Church must attend precisely because the Church "realizes that it is exposed to fierce temptations as it speaks of God, and it realizes that it must give an account to God for the way in which it speaks."[97] It is this accounting that Barth's *Realdialektik* takes most seriously. It is significant that the passage from *CD* I.2 that Hooke finds objectionable is taken from the paragraph in which Barth is arguing for "Pure Doctrine as the Problem of Dogmatics." For Barth, the preacher cannot simply move from exegesis to performance in a two-step process that circumvents the critical questions dogmatics would pose to the *content* of the proposed sermon. The same paragraph of *CD* reminds us that dogmatics "is *in concreto* the effort and concern of the Church for the purity of its doctrine. Its problem is essentially *the* problem of preaching."[98] The structure of the performance course Hooke describes appears to bypass the dogmatic theological task altogether. "The upshot of (Barth's) argument, *for a theology of preaching*," she states, "is that the success of preaching does not depend at all on the actions of the preacher—the quality of her sermon, the depth of her insight, her personal presence, whether what she is saying means anything to her."[99] But this is simply not the case, for as Barth makes clear, there is plenty of work for the preacher to do. The preacher's post-exegetical work, however, lies primarily in the field of dogmatics, *not* that of performance.

> The grace of the Word of God is not magic. It is promised to the Church that is required and ready to serve it. If it makes strong what men make weak, good what men make evil, pure what men make impure, that does not mean that it does everything where men do simply nothing, where men perhaps do not stand under this requirement and in this readiness. When we have done all that was required of us, we must add that we are but unprofitable servants.[100]

Here Barth has anticipated my *third* point. While Hooke begins by criticizing Barth's doctrine of revelation from the point of view of

97. Barth, *CD* 1/1:3.
98. Barth, *CD* 1/2:766; emphasis mine.
99. Hooke, "'I Am Here in this Room . . .'", 14; emphasis mine.
100. Barth, *CD* 1/2:765–66.

the Incarnation, she seems to conflate the latter with anthropology. But if the Incarnation is to instruct us in matters of revelation, as Hooke rightly insists (and Barth well understood), then the *particularity* of "God's paradigmatic event of self-revelation, the incarnation, life, death and resurrection of Jesus Christ," must be respected. In other words, the one whom we know as "God with us," the one who, "though *he* was in the form of God, did not regard equality with God as something to be exploited, but emptied himself, taking the form of a slave" (2:7), *he* did *not* say to us, "*You* are worthless slaves." Rather, he graciously taught *us* to *say to ourselves*: "'*We* are worthless slaves; we have done only what we ought to have done!'" (Luke 17:10) This, I would suggest, is what Barth meant when he spoke of the (inseparable) dialectic of grace and judgment, that is, in terms of "obedience to grace."

> Theology as a science . . . would be meaningless without justifying grace, which here too can alone make good what man as such invariably does badly. But it can be meaningful as an act of obedience to this grace, i.e., of the obedience in which here too man may believe that he is doing well even though he does not see it. . . . The Church produces theology in this special and peculiar sense *by subjecting itself to self-examination.* . . . Theology accompanies the utterance of the Church to the extent that it is itself no more than "talk about God," so that with this talk *it stands under the judgment that begins at the house of God* and *lives by the promise* given to the Church.[101]

At some point, I expect Hooke's thesis would benefit by taking seriously Barth's critique of the self as distinct from the body, or for that matter, Kierkegaard's definition of the self as spirit.[102] A feminine perspective surely has many important insights to share with regard to the body's role in a proper anthropological understanding of the self, but a critique of Barth's view of the self must first recognize that his critique is not of the body. On the contrary, one could well argue that such a principle of acting, which presupposes that the preacher can be somehow less than fully present, or less than human, when her body is in the room, has a far greater disembodying effect than does Barth's notion of transparency.[103]

101. Barth, *CD* 1/1:4, emphasis mine; see also McCormack, *CRDT*, 17–18.
102. Kierkegaard, *Sickness unto Death*, 13–14.
103. Hooke, "'I Am Here in this Room . . .'", 20.

Fourth, there is the interdisciplinary question. Hooke's turn from Barth's theology to Gadamer's philosophical hermeneutics appears uncritical and premature at this point, and misses out on what might actually prove helpful in the development of a performance theory. Barth's well-known understanding of the interpretative task involves the three steps of *explicatio*, *meditatio*, and *applicatio*. As mentioned above, where the structure of the Yale performance course and Barth appear to disconnect most radically is with regard to the intermediate dogmatic enterprise. In other words, "the middle point between *sensus* and *usus*, (between) *explicatio* and *applicatio*" seems to have been bypassed, though it offers a much more sympathetic understanding of the interpretive task than we might expect. Barth not only concedes the fact that the reader/observer cannot escape his or her epistemological particularity—"Everyone has some philosophy"—he fairly insists upon it, fully expecting the interpreter to engage in exploration and experimentation.[104] The question is neither whether the use of a particular (i.e., emphatically biblical!) hermeneutical approach can be avoided, nor whether it will influence the reading, but the crucial question for Barth is *how* will it do so?

In answer to this question, Barth offers five guidelines for this *reflective* stage of interpretation: (1) We must know what we are doing. "We must be very clear that every scheme of thought which we bring with us is different from that of the scriptural word which we have to interpret, for the object of the latter is God's revelation in Jesus Christ, it is the testimony of this revelation inspired by the Holy Ghost, and it can become luminous for us only through the same Holy Ghost. Our philosophy as such . . . stands always in contrast to the philosophy of scripture."[105]

(2) The "manner of thought we bring with us . . . can only have the fundamental character of a hypothesis." Yet this, for Barth, is a sign of the *freedom*, which *every member of the Church* enjoys, to "apply this way of thought to the problems of Scripture, in an exploratory and experimental and provisional way." While interpretation must always take seriously our human particularities, we must also expect the Word to radically transform our epistemological categories. Therefore, I exercise

104. Barth, *CD* 1/2:727–30.
105. Ibid., 730.

my freedom with the full recognition that "it will be decided under the Word what becomes of my mode of thought."[106]

(3) Our interpretative approach, our "hermeneutic," if we must, must never "become an end in itself." Rather, we must remember that philosophy poses an ever-present danger to scriptural exegesis. To put it in terms of "the infinite qualitative difference," the danger occurs when human wisdom claims too much for itself over against the divine wisdom revealed in Scripture. Barth does not banish philosophy, but merely places it under the proper constraints.

> It [philosophy] obviously becomes dangerous when in using it we cease to be aware of its difference from the biblical way of thought and its original unfitness for the apprehension and interpretation of the latter. It becomes dangerous when we consider it to be a fit and adequate instrument for this purpose. It becomes dangerous, therefore, when—even with the best intention, that of doing justice to Scripture—we posit it absolutely over against Scripture, expecting that by placing it, as it were, on the same high level as Scripture, we can use it to control Scripture.[107]

(4) Barth sees "no essential reason for preferring one of these schemes [of interpretive thought] to another." Human hermeneutical, epistemological, and philosophical schemes will certainly need to be adjudicated, but they will not, of themselves, transcend their strictly human quality. Barth asks, "How can we bind ourselves to one philosophy as the only philosophy, and ascribe to it a universal necessity, without actually positing it as something absolute as the necessary partner of the Word of God and in that way imprisoning and falsifying the Word of God?"[108]

(5) Barth again affirms the legitimacy and fruitfulness of our use of such interpretive schemes of thought *when* they are "determined and controlled by the text and the object mirrored in the text," in other words, by the second and first forms of the Word of God, respectively. In short, the crucial point for Barth in all of these guidelines is that the Word—incarnate, yes, but divinely revealed—sets the guidelines.

---

106. Ibid., 730–31.
107. Ibid., 731–32.
108. Ibid., 733.

For this reason, theories of preaching that would be informed by dramatic principles must do better than simply turn from dogmatics in order to receive baptism at the hands of esthetics, philosophy, or hermeneutics, especially where these deny or diminish the transcendent and trade in strictly horizontal, anthropological categories such as race, class, gender, culture, categories that, in a certain theologically dialectical sense, no longer hold for those who in faith are to be found "in Christ."[109] I would argue that the case for interdisciplinary "borrowing" from the theatre would have to be made from the perspective of scripture and theology, which, precisely due to their theological subject matter, have certain critical and corrective things to say to the non-theological disciplines, including both the arts and sciences. Only in this way can the corrective be supplied that the Word and Spirit alone are able to provide. The strength of Barth's cautionary admonitions notwithstanding, it is important to recall that he locates these guidelines for interpretive reflection under the rubric of *freedom*, which is nevertheless "freedom *under* the Word."

Finally, Hooke repeatedly describes Barth's concern that the preacher not be granted "too much power" in quantitative terms. At issue, however, is not so much power as authority and, again, the distinctions should remain qualitative. First and foremost, Barth understands authority as accruing to God absolutely. Second, with respect to his doctrine of the Word, he treats the question of authority (always in dialectical relation to freedom) most explicitly in his chapter on Holy Scripture, in which we are reminded that Scripture bestows both authority and freedom *on* the Church, but also exerts both authority and freedom *over* the Church. With respect to proclamation, however, *authority* tends to be restated in terms of the *heteronomy* that pertains to dogmatic *norms* and the *autonomy* that pertains to dogmatic *thinking*.

According to *DGD*, *heteronomy* requires that dogmatics "measure the human word of preaching by the Word of God which is supposed

---

109. I am thinking of any number of presbytery meetings I have attended wherein Gal 3:27–28—"There is no longer Jew or Greek, . . . slave or free, . . . male or female; for all of you are one in Christ Jesus"—is used liturgically in services of commissioning, only to turn and receive reports from racial-ethnic caucuses and Presbyterian women, all of whom unquestionably are engaged in very diverse, important, and instrumental ministries. Nevertheless, on such occasions, one cannot help but wonder, "What happened to 'no longer'?" Similarly, the endless specialization of hermeneutics, it seems to me, swiftly arrives at the point of absurdity.

to be spoken in it," by keeping in view (1) canonical, (2) confessional, and (3) Church norms. What is interesting here is that in *DGD*, Barth introduces the topic of heteronomy both in terms of the *Realdialektik* of *Romans* II and in terms of his *method* of dialectical thinking. It is here that we find the original quotation, paraphrased by Migliore, in which Barth muses, "Only in heaven, [will we] no longer have any need of dialectic."[110] Here also, Barth sees fit to drop in the passage from Ecclesiastes 5:2. "God is in heaven and you upon earth."[111]

Dialectic is explained even more explicitly in Barth's treatment of *"the autonomy of dogmatic thinking"* in terms of *"the autonomy of the Holy Spirit."*[112] His definition of *autonomy* also takes a three-fold form. It requires that dogmatic thinking always be: (1) *"the thinking of faith and obedience,"* (2) *"human thinking which at all costs has to orient itself to its theme,"* and (3) *"the thinking of individuals who see themselves set before this theme."* It is the second point that calls for an explicit definition of dialectic.

> What does dialectic mean? To put it innocuously and in a way that should awaken confidence, *dialektein* means to converse with others, to deal with them, to discuss with them. Dialectic means, then, thinking in such a way that there is dialogue. Two are needed for this. There must be two incompatible but inseparable partners in my thinking: a word and a counter-word, for example, faith and obedience, authority and freedom, God and man, grace and sin, inside and outside, etc. How does the counter-word, and therefore the dialogue, come to have a place in my thinking? First I think pious words before God that are nondialectically neutral, as ought to happen in the thinking of obedience and faith. I even try to think about God himself with these words of mine. But I cannot succeed. For every time, on the one side, when I believe that I have thought about God, I remember that God is subject, not object. I have to turn around, then, and think radically, on the other side, whence I came in order to do this. When this situation is seen again at any point there arises the dialectical relation of two concepts. Dialogue takes the place

110. Barth, *DGD*, 285–86.

111. Though Barth inserted only this abbreviated portion of the verse in question, the entire verse should be kept in mind, which reads: "Never be rash with your mouth, nor let your heart be quick to utter a word before God, for God is in heaven, and you upon earth; therefore let your words be few" (Eccl 5:2).

112. Barth, *DGD*, 289.

in this relation, and to that extent, like all dogmatic thinking, it
is dialectical dialogue. Thinking nondialectically would mean in
principle not thinking before God. Before God human thoughts
become dialectical.[113]

Here we have an explicit statement of the dialogical, or better, yet
conversational character of dialectic that our initial lexical investiga-
tion in §1 suggested. Clearly, Barth's theology of preaching, which is so
thoroughly attentive to dialectic, is already inherently and essentially
conversational. In this respect, Gadamer's conversational hermeneutic
offers nothing which is not already there in Barth. On the other hand,
while both Barth's statements on heteronomy and autonomy pertain

---

113. Ibid., 309–11. Frankly, I find Barth somewhat scripturally weak at this point,
since in the New Testament, *dialogismos* (n) and *dialogizesthai* (v) are consistently used
of parties or in situations wherein parties (such as the scribes and Pharisees, and even
the disciples) respond with skepticism (Matt 16:7–8; Mark 2:6, 8; 8:16–17; Luke 5:21–22;
24:38), "evil intentions" (Matt 15:19; Mark 7:21; Luke 6:7–8; 9:46–47; 12:17; 20:14; John
11:50; Jas 2:4), futile thinking and senseless arguments (Matt 21:25; Mark 9:33; 11:31;
Rom 1:21; 14:1; 1 Cor 3:20; Phil 2:14; 1 Tim 2:8). Only on three occurrences is the term
used with something approaching neutrality (Luke 1:29; 2:35; 3:15) to portray perplexity and confusion; but remarkably, the root word *dialog-* is never once commended in
the New Testament. By contrast, *dialegesthai* (v), whence *dialectic* is derived, is used
repeatedly to describe Paul's itinerant preaching ministry of persuasive and forceful
argumentation "from the scriptures" in the synagogues (Acts 17:2, 17; 18:4, 19; 19:8),
as well as in the lecture hall of Tyrannus (19:9); in his less formal, but evidently urgent
discussions in Troas (20:7, 9); and in his testimony before Felix (24:12, 25), though
admittedly the first of these latter two uses occurs in Paul's denial of having engaged in
any such "disputes" or stirred up a crowd. The term is used only three times outside the
Book of Acts. The unique occurrence in the gospels is in Mark, where the term finds
negative use in describing the disciples *debating* who was the greatest (9:34). In a startling instance in Jude, *dialegeto* is used of the archangel Michael's disputing and *arguing*
with the devil over the body of Moses (v. 9). Not least importantly, in Hebrews the word
is used in reminding the readers of the "exhortation that *addresses* you as children—
'My child, do not regard lightly the discipline of the Lord, or lose heart when you are
punished by him'" (12:5). Although few of these uses of the term occur in especially
pleasant circumstances, all but one or two of the dozen occurrences describe difficult
but necessary contestation, usually missionary or (so-called) "militant" preaching of
the gospel. In short, the New Testament views *dialectic* far more postively than *dialog-*,
which has not simply evolved along an etymological trajectory but mutated into something quite contrary to its original sense, taking on, in the English word *dialogue*, the
benign and benevolent characteristics of a universal panacea for every problem under
the sun, and finding wide use in liturgical literature to describe the encounter with God
in worship. One wonders, however, in light of the New Testament, if *dialogue* is the
appropriate term to describe what God has at stake in the service of worship and in the
proclamation of the gospel.

to what Migliore sees as Barth's *dialectical method*, what must not be missed is the fact that the *diastasis* is clearly operative in both as well, that is, along the vertical axis. Dialectical theology brings the conversation "before God" and orients itself to God "at all costs."

In sum, the implications of *diastasis* for a theory of preaching performance is that the latter must finally answer the question: how does preaching, understood as the Word of God, differ from theatre or from esthetics in general? Does not preaching require a "wholly other" type of "performance," one that is altogether *qualitatively* different from acting and drama, one that requires an apostolic work of love uniquely and distinctly inspired by and attributable to the Holy Spirit? Further, does this qualitative difference not have everything to do with the difference between, on the one hand, human imagination and humanly perceived reality, and on the other hand, that which Barth understood as God's "real reality," that which is only revealed in the dialectic of objectively real relations that *precede and remain autonomous from* human perception, wisdom, knowledge, experience, and imagination? Finally, is it not the reality of this "infinite qualitative difference" and the recognition that we are utterly at the mercy of an *autonomous* Holy Spirit (John 3:8) that necessitates we "test everything" (1 Thess 5:21) and "pray without ceasing" (5:17)? Again, I would hold that the *diastasis* is *the* presupposition of the Christian revelation, respecting but transcending all particularistic hermeneutical claims, and unless we wrongly ascribe autonomy to ourselves rather than to the Holy Spirit, we will see in it the reason why true preaching depends absolutely on the Spirit's response to *epiclesis* and *invocation*.

§3. A Pedagogical Exercise

§3.1 *The Purpose*

The pedagogical exercise I propose is quite modest. Its aim is to help preaching students to recognize: (1) the pervasive feature of the *diastasis*, the infinite qualitative difference between God and human beings, eternity and time, heaven and earth, revelation and hiddenness; (2) that this feature is identified in the New Testament itself, on *both* sides of Easter, as the primary test of biblical interpretation, or in other words, the presupposition on which further discernment depends; and (3) that when Barth's *analogia fidei* is identified, that is, where *pistis*—whether translated faith, belief, or trust—determines a favorable result or clear discernment, it too functions dialectically.

§3.2 *The Exercise*

The pedagogical exercise proposed here is as follows:

1. Students (either individually outside of class or as a group in a classroom setting) should be asked to read straight through the Gospel of Mark in a "Red Letter edition," skipping all the black letters. In other words, read through the speeches of Jesus in the Gospel of Mark in a single sitting. (In order to avoid rushing through the material, no less than 30 minutes should be reserved for the reading itself.)

2. Prior to the reading, state the question the students are to keep before them as the speeches are read. The instructor may wish to display the question visually for the duration of the reading. If the instructor prefers to make the question open-ended, it should be stated as follows: *Is there a recurrent distinction being made in the content of the sayings attributed to Jesus?* Or the instructor may wish to state the question more explicitly: *How many statements can you identify in which Jesus says, in effect: "God's ways are not human ways," that is, where a distinction is being drawn between the divine and the human, between heaven and earth?*

3. A secondary question might also be asked: *How many additional statements can be identified in which* pistis *(faith, belief, or trust) plays a decisive role in revealing God's actions as opposed to human expectations?*

4. Have students record the results of their search and share their findings, either in class discussion, or in rough, tabulated form, though preferably not as an essay.

§3.3 *Rationale*

> *For my thoughts are not your thoughts,*
> *nor are your ways my ways,* says the LORD.
> *For as the heavens are higher than the earth,*
> *so are my ways higher than your ways*

and my thoughts than your thoughts. (Isa 55:8–9)

The exercise proposed here focusses primarily on the Gospel of Mark, though it could certainly be modified for use with Pauline (e.g., 1 Cor 1–4), Johannine, or a wide variety of other texts (Job 32–42; Eccl 5–8; Isa 55; et al.). I suggest Mark for several reasons. First, quite simply, Mark is brief. Second, the fact that the Markan material is included in both Matthew and Luke will serve as an assurance that the dialectic under observation is not peculiar to Mark alone. Third, as Mark (sometimes considered the "earthiest" gospel) will, to a degree, represent the synoptic tradition, we will not be seen to be appealing to the stereotypically "dualistic" elements often attributed to John, although it is these very elements which I suggest need to be understood anew, that is, *dialectically*, in terms of God's "wholly otherness." Fourth, focusing in particular on the speeches of Jesus in the shared synoptic material will take us over the very ground that was worked by the New Hermeneutic and the New Homiletic when these schools took to the study of parables under the presupposition that parabolic form was characteristic of *how* Jesus preached.[114]

In advancing the present Barthian/Kierkegaardian proposal, we can certainly appreciate many historical insights gained by these schools. I am nevertheless convinced that the attempt to determine "whether Jesus really said it" is fruitless and vacuous. On the other hand, neither historical, narrative, literary, nor post-structuralist critics can deny that the determination to attribute certain words to Jesus can only have been made—regardless of who (humanly speaking) made the determination—with a sense of their particular weight and authority.[115]

---

114. The methodological assumption that the sayings of Jesus in the earliest gospel may be taken as "core gospel" may be viewed with suspicion from either of two perspectives. First, the quest for the historical Jesus, itself suspicious of many of the sayings attributed to Jesus, is in turn regarded as suspect by those who deny the possibility or even the appropriateness of isolating a core set of passages within the larger canon. In this respect, a "red letter" reading may well be seen as doubly dubious, that is, to source critics who would dismiss such an approach as historically simplistic and open to contextual misapplication, as well as to biblicists who seek to avoid, though never with much success, privileging any one biblical passage above another. Here we venture the naive reading.

115. This is not to advocate a *textus receptus* approach *per se*. McCormack has reminded us that Barth "backed off from advocating a *textus receptus* in the *Church Dogmatics*." McCormack, *CRDT*, 347; see also Barth, *CD* 1/2:602–3.

§3.3.1 A RETURN TO CONTENT

With the focus on *form* that gave impetus to the development of narrative preaching, the New Homiletic effectively headed off any further
inquiry into dogmatic challenges to sermon *content* by claiming that,
by virtue of a McLuhanesque unity of form and content (a unity which
is, of course, undeniable in the person of Jesus Christ), such inquiries
would only arrive at the same destination. As we have seen in Buttrick's
sermon rationale, which he associates directly with Craddock's approach, the preacher of parables is to "let *the structural movement* of
the parable do its intended work."[116] This is, of course, a significant
departure from the Lutheran principle in which the preacher is to "let
the Word do its work,"[117] because the New Homiletic assumes a unity
between form and content which Luther never presupposed. Elsewhere,
I have questioned the New Homiletic's assumption that a unity between
form and content can be derived from Christology and directly applied
as a homiletical principle.[118] Here, I continue to regard with suspicion
the assumption that any dichotomy that separates *form* from *content*
is a false one. Objections to the New Hermeneutic's fixation on parable, of course, have come from many other quarters as well. One of the
most important has been registered by Paul J. Achtemeier, who observes
that the New Hermeneutic is not equipped to explain or interpret the
miracles of Jesus (without simply dismissing them).[119] I would contend
that Barth was much closer to identifying a normative mode of biblical interpretation than the New Hermeneutic, one that is equally well
equipped to deal with parable and miracle, as well as other narrative and
rhetorical forms, when he insisted that biblical interpretation depends
entirely upon the *content* of scripture. In a very important passage from
the aforementioned heading "Freedom under the Word," Barth explains
the necessity of deriving our interpretive presuppositions from the content of scripture itself. It merits a lengthy quotation.

---

116. Buttrick, *CV,* 98.

117. Gritsch, "Luther, Martin," 315.

118. The attempt to apply the ideal unity of form and content in Jesus Christ to a
homiletical method fails precisely because it ignores the "infinite qualitative difference"
between the preacher and the sermon, on the one hand, and the Word of God incarnate
in Jesus Christ, on the other. See Slemmons, "Penitential Homiletic."

119. Achtemeier, *Introduction to the New Hermeneutic.*

Scriptural exegesis rests on the assumption that *the message which Scripture has to give us, even in its apparently most debatable and least assimilable parts, is in all circumstances truer and more important than the best and most necessary things that we ourselves have said or can say.* In that it is the divinely ordained and authorised witness to revelation, it has the claim to be interpreted in this sense, and if this claim be not duly heeded, it remains at bottom inexplicable. *The Bible is outwardly,* so to speak, *accessible only from a certain point below. Therefore we must take our stand at that point below, in order to look up to the corresponding point above.*[120]

The decisive basis of this fundamental rule of all scriptural exegesis can be inferred, of course, only from the *content* of Scripture, and only from there can it become really intelligible. Why must we subordinate the testimony of our own spirit to the testimony of the spirit of Scripture? Why do we have this particular assumption which is so obviously out of accord with the technique of interpretation generally? . . . We will leave aside for the moment what we have already established earlier in another connexion—that perhaps the technique of interpretation generally . . . has every cause to learn from the special biblical science of interpretation which in the last resort is the only possible one. There will be reasons for the fact that it does not desire, and is not able, to do this. But it is certain that biblical hermeneutics must be controlled by this fundamental principle because the *content* of the Bible imperatively requires it. *The content of the Bible, and the object of its witness, is Jesus Christ as the name of the God who deals graciously with man the sinner.* . . . To hear this is to hear the Bible—both as a whole and in each one of its separate parts. Not to hear this means *eo ipso* not to hear the Bible, neither as a whole, nor therefore in its parts. The Bible says all sorts of things, certainly; but in all this multiplicity and variety, it says in truth only one thing—just this: the name of Jesus Christ, concealed under the name Israel in the Old Testament, revealed under His own name in the New Testament, which therefore can be understood only as it has understood itself, as a commentary on the Old Testament. The Bible becomes clear when it is clear that it says this one thing: that it proclaims the name Jesus Christ and therefore proclaims God in His richness and mercy, and man in his need and helplessness, yet living on what God's mercy has given and will give

120. Barth, *CD* 1/2:719; emphasis mine.

him. The Bible remains dark to us if we do not hear in it this sovereign name, and if, therefore, we think we perceive God and man in some other relation than the one determined once for all by this name. *Interpretation stands in service of the clarity which the Bible as God's Word makes for itself; and we can properly interpret the Bible, in whole or in part, only when we perceive and show that what it says is said from the point of view of that concealed and revealed name of Jesus Christ, and therefore, in testimony to the grace of which we stand in need, of which as men we are incapable and of which we are made participants by God. From this is to be inferred the basic principle of the subordination of our ideas, thoughts, and conviction to the testimony of Scripture itself. Our own ideas, thoughts, and convictions as such, as ours, certainly do not run in the direction of the testimony which has this particular content.* . . . But if the Word of God has actually come into its own, and if it is to be clearly seen, the only thing which can happen to the world of thought which exposes the nature of man is that it should at least give ground (for we cannot simply free ourselves from it, nor ought we to try to do so, since emancipation from it is identical with the resurrection of the flesh), that it should become fluid, losing its absoluteness, *subordinating itself and following the Word as a tamed beast of prey must follow its master.*[121]

In contrast to the clarity of which Barth speaks here, albeit in terms of the dialectic of revelation and hiddenness, what is remarkable about the overwhelming attention narrative theory has given to the *form* of the parable is the readiness with which such interpretation contents itself with and normalizes the form and movement of Jesus' teaching that applies to and excludes the un-discerning outsider (Mark 4:11–12). Despite the clear indication that Jesus intends for the disciples to understand the parables (Mark 4:11, 13) and goes to great lengths to "explain" them to the disciples "in private" (Mark 4:33–34; 7:17–23), narrative preaching has, in effect, ruled out the possibility of acquiring an understanding of the *content* of the parables that can be clearly distinguished from their parabolic *form*, first, by largely ignoring the private explanations, and second, by ruling out the authenticity of the given interpretations, either by shrinking from their humble allegory or on dubious source-critical grounds, that is, ruling out the report of the

---

121. Ibid., 719–21; emphasis mine. With respect to interpretation that attempts to follow, *with fluidity*, the "spiritual logic" of the Word, see my essay, "Synkrinesis."

explanations to insiders based on what amounts to a privileged insider knowledge of the sources, claimed at a distance of two millennia no less, and finally, by reconciling this lack of insider information by equating form with content, or in a sense, by demanding that the interpreter satisfy himself with the parabolic form of the revelation. While I do not pretend piously to be an "insider" or suggest the insider is invulnerable to the workings of parable that conceal meaning as readily as they reveal it, I *do* mean to uphold the plain sense of the text according to which the disciples *were* given explanations that cannot be simplistically reduced to a rationalization for scholarly incomprehension, or disguised in the false garb of a unity of form and content. In short, there *is* an "insider" understanding to be sought. *Of course* this understanding is still subject to the dialectic of hiddenness and revelation, but this dialectic is not confined to parable, neither is it open to "doubt" or to the doubter who would challenge the authority of the Word.

Faith, or Barth's *analogia fidei* (which, as McCormack has reminded us, functions dialectically) is precisely the God-given means by which one becomes an insider (if we must put it this way) or is initiated into the follow-able "logic of the Spirit."[122] In Kierkegaardian terms, faith is infinitely, qualitatively higher than a form-focussed, consumeristic esthetic. It is the sphere that completely transcends the immanent sphere in which form is regarded objectively. In short, the assertion that form and content are one belongs to the esthetic sphere, wherein faith is *not* exercised by the observing subject with the result that the interpreter is *always* an outsider, always excluded. In order to gain the interior, however, in order to enter the sphere of faith, the interpreter must first become conscious of sin and of himself as a sinner, over against that which he is not, namely, the sinless, crucified God-man, who is the Sovereign Truth. Entrance into the sphere of faith by "the leap" inescapably elicits *epiclesis*—the prayer for divine deliverance—the very plea by which one becomes subject to this Man of Truth, Jesus Christ, first of all, by not taking offense at him, and second, by recognizing and leaping in faith the abyss that lies between the sinless, eternal, infinite God and the sinful, temporal, finite human being.

As I understand it, this abyss, this radical discontinuity, is inseparable from what McCormack terms the *diastasis* in Barth. It is, however,

---

122. See Slemmons, "*Synkrinesis*," as well as the important book by Loder, *The Logic of the Spirit*.

what the New Homiletic either routinely ignores or presumes to be able to eliminate with introductions (Buttrick) or ingenious parables of the preacher's own devising (Craddock). If we turn to Jesus' words in the Gospel of Mark, however, we find this very discontinuity emerging as a primary, if not *the* primary presupposition. In what follows, I will first show that the Markan parables themselves must be read dialectically. Second, I will gather together those sayings that self-evidently call attention to this *diastasis*. Third, I will only briefly gather, without elaborating upon them, those sayings that reveal this diastasis by way of the *analogia fidei*.

§3.3.2 A Relative Dearth of Parable

Oddly enough, though Jesus speaks in every chapter of Mark (assuming that the longer ending is not thrown out entirely), parable as such is only mentioned explicitly in five of Mark's sixteen chapters (3, 4, 7, 12, and 13). What does Jesus say in all those *other* chapters? We will get to that later. Not surprisingly, however, when we consider the parabolic passages with our dialectical eyes open, we find that the necessarily disputatious sense of the term emerges in a startling way, one that not only reveals the "infinite qualitative difference" between heaven and earth, but also suggests homiletical fascination with parable may be an elaborate way for modern religious authorities to avoid the implications of the dialectic!

Mark 7:14–15, for instance, refers to one specific parabolic saying that summarizes a lengthy debate with "the Pharisees and some of the scribes" (7:1–13) and includes an interpretation given to insiders (7:17–23). To narrow in on this "parable," however, is a distraction from the content of the preceding and thoroughly dialectical *debate* with the religious authorities, a debate that clearly arises from the reading exercise proposed here. In this debate Jesus makes an open declaration of the problem in the baldest possible terms, namely, the substitution of human wisdom for divine revelation. The confrontation is a direct attack on human tradition, which, though couched in the gospel narrative, takes a diastatic, not a parabolic form.

> He said to them, "Isaiah prophesied rightly about you hypocrites, as it is written, 'This people honors me with their lips, but their hearts are far from me; in vain do they worship me, *teaching*

human precepts as doctrines.' You abandon the commandment of God and hold to human tradition." Then he said to them, "*You have a fine way of rejecting the commandment of God in order to keep your tradition!* For Moses said, 'Honor your father and your mother'; and, 'Whoever speaks evil of father or mother must surely die.' But you say that if anyone tells father or mother, 'Whatever support you might have had from me is Corban' (that is, an offering to God)—then you no longer permit doing anything for a father or mother, *thus making void the word of God through your tradition that you have handed on. And you do many things like this.*" (Mark 7:6–13; emphasis mine)

Here the abandonment of the sacred ethic of familial responsibility, an ethic entirely in keeping with the will of God, is but one example of the ways in which human tradition ignores divine justice and then attempts to pin the blame on God, as if God would ever desire worship at the expense of compassion and justice. We must not, however, lose the content of the issue in the form of the argument. The form makes use of an *example*, followed by the observation, "And you do many things like this" (v. 13). But Jesus does not waste time naming all possible examples of such behavior, as if one must speak inclusively of all diverse contexts in which such abuses take place. The issue does not warrant getting bogged down in innumerable anecdotes, situational ethics, or endless horizontal (human) comparisons. It can only be properly discerned vertically: human tradition in *diastasis* with the commands of God.

While Mark 12:1a refers to Jesus' speaking in parables in the plural sense, it includes only one specific parable (12:1b–11), that of the wicked tenants, and the report of the angry reaction it provoked (12:12)—but from *whom?* Mark 12:12 refers only to "they." We must return to Mark 11:27, in order to discover who the angry listeners were: "the chief priests, the scribes, and the elders" who came to him demanding, "By what authority are you doing these things?" Here again, the methodological moral of the New Homiletic, "Jesus preached in parables," if it draws our attention strictly to the parable proper, allows the antagonists, and *the fact that they are the religious authorities*, to slip into the shadows. Indeed, our "red letter" approach also bypasses, or more precisely, presumes a prior knowledge (on the part of seminary students) of important contextual material as well. Nevertheless, this debate (11:27–33) will figure prominently in a dialectical reading of Jesus' sayings in Mark, even if the words of Jesus must, for the time being, function rhetorically all on their own. It is, in fact, one of the most revealing discourses of all, and one of the most important for biblical interpretation. We recall the challenge to Jesus' authority takes place in the temple. His reply to their challenge, issued in the presence of God no less, is as follows:

> I will ask you one question; answer me, and I will tell you by what authority I do these things. Did the baptism of John come from heaven, or was it of human origin? Answer me. (Mark 11:29–30)

If there was ever a time for the dialectician to chime in with Ecclesiastes 5:1–2, it is now! "Guard your steps when you go to the house of God; to draw near to listen is better than the sacrifice offered by fools; . . . Never be rash with your mouth, nor let your heart be quick to utter a word before God; for God is in heaven and you upon earth; therefore let your words be few" (Eccl 5:1–2; cf. Mark 12:40). The authorities are more concerned with what the crowd will think than they are concerned that "the LORD is in his holy temple" (Ps 11:4; Hab 2:20) awaiting their reply. By dropping the account of the scribes' inconclusive huddle, however, the readers of red letters only have the question put even more directly to them. "Heaven or earth? Up or down? Which one is it? The Lord awaits your answer." Or, as I often paraphrase the question to those who live in a post-modern world that has long since grown too sophisticated for a three-tiered universe: "Do you even know which way is up? If you do not, then what more can you expect Jesus to say? If we do not know which way is up, how can he begin to explain to us whence his authority derives? Authority is from above, is it not? But if we don't know what 'above' means, well, where to begin?"

As with the specific examples Jesus cites in the debate of Mark 7, the particularity of his reply must not overtake the reader's ability to identify the universal. A historical critical hermeneutic would investigate the perceptions the religious authorities of the day had of John the Baptist, and reconstruct what that particular question would have meant to those particular authorities in that particular context. Fortunately, the narrator has done that work for the reader (11:31–32), who is left to consider Jesus' question. Neither is this simply a trivia quiz, a brainteaser, or a trick question designed to stump them. Read dialectically, Jesus is simply asking them, "Are you teachable? If you cannot or will not discern the difference between the heavenly and the human, then you will not understand anything more I would say to you." In fact, having discerned precisely what was at stake, the authorities in the text still refuse to answer. Like the demons in Mark's gospel, who are the first to identify Jesus yet remain in the service of Satan, these authorities know the truth cognitively, but can not, or will not, risk faith in the authority that proceeds from a heavenly origin. In fact, the authorities themselves chose to end the discussion. Jesus simply calls it closed in terms that indicate they will receive no further revelation: "Neither will I tell you by what authority I am doing these things" (11:33).

The parable of the divided house (3:23–26) is also nested in the context of a fiery debate with the scribes who charge Jesus with using the power of Beelzebul to cast out demons (3:19b–30). At issue is the discernment of spirits (1 John 4:1; 1 Cor 1:19; 2:15; 12:10). Here too, just outside the parable proper, Jesus declares, in the most sobering dialectical terms, that the unforgivable sin is blasphemy against the Holy Spirit, the attributing of a divine, blessed miracle to the prince of demons. In other words, these wicked scribes "call evil good and good evil" (Isa 5:20).

The parable of the fig tree in Mark 13:28–29 is set, not in the context of a debate, but in that of Mark's "little apocalypse" (Mark 13:1–37). More specifically, it occurs between the *vertical* eschatological prophesy that "they will see 'the Son of Man coming in clouds'" (13:26) and the radically dialectical claim that, regarding the "day and the hour" of these end time events, "no one knows, neither the angels in heaven, nor the Son, but only the Father" (Mark 13:32). Further, the "lesson" (*parabolen*) itself contains what appears to be a dialectically definitive statement, one that claims for Jesus' words an absolutely eternal quality such that the heaven-and-earth dialectic itself must bow to them as sovereign and eternal and be reframed as temporal by comparison: "Heaven and earth will pass away, but my words will never pass away" (13:31).

Apart from these four episodic parables, in only one chapter of Mark do we find a dense concentration of parables.[123] Mark 4 is almost entirely devoted to Jesus' parables. As I have treated this chapter in some detail elsewhere,[124] I will not do so again here, except to note that one

---

123. To some this list may seem to short, as it does not gather all aphoristic sayings (2:19–22; 25–28; 9:35, et al.) under the rubric of parable.

124. Slemmons, "*Synkrinesis.*"

of its parables makes mention of an "insider" interpretation (4:10–20), while the parabolic section of the chapter ends with another report of such private disclosure: "With many such parables he spoke the word to them, as they were able to hear it; he did not speak to them except in parables, *but he explained everything in private to his disciples*" (Mark 4:33–34).

Significantly, the only non-parable in this chapter is an account of a miracle in which Jesus calms a storm, after which the disciples respond with awe, even terror (*ephobethesan phobon megan*), saying to one another, "Who then is this, that even the wind and the sea obey him?" (Mark 4:42) This miracle story perhaps more properly belongs to those passages in which the *analogia fidei* would be determinative of revelation and understanding, in light of Jesus' question: "Why are you afraid? Have you still no faith?" (4:40). I mention it here, however, in order to complete this consideration of the explicitly parabolic sections in Mark.

§3.3.3 SET YOUR MIND ON DIVINE THINGS!

We have identified the *diastasis* at work in intimate proximity to the Markan parables, and observed that, while there are relatively few parables in Mark, focussing on the parables themselves finally limits interpretation by leading the reader away from the dialectic, which often occurs, not surprisingly, in the context of an argument. There is no dearth of dialectical sayings, however, in the remaining chapters of Mark. Without claiming to offer an exhaustive summary here, I would nevertheless survey some of the primary instances in which the *diastasis* emerges most clearly.

Jesus' rebuke of the apostle Peter (Mark 8:31–33) is one such primary instance. "Get behind me, Satan! For you are setting your mind not on divine things but on human things" (Mark 8:33; but see also 8:34–38; 9:1). The particular question at issue here is Jesus' destiny. Will he become a "hero" to the satisfaction of a natural human desire for the esthetically happy ending, or will he be rejected, scourged, go to the cross, and suffer death in accordance with the humanly and ethically unthinkable will of God? This is, again, embedded in the most important narrative in human history, but even the momentous particularity of this singular event does not preclude our understanding the rebuke in all its universality. To focus on human things to the exclusion, confusion, ignorance, refusal, or the denial of the will of God is downright diabolical. Even the very first "pope" was fallible and he did not lose an instant in demonstrating it (Matt 16:13–20). It is tempting at this point to appeal to Matthew, where Peter's confession as to the identity of Jesus (which, in both gospels, immediately precedes Peter's "fall,") meets with a strong dialectical affirmation of his divine inspiration: "Blessed are you, Simon son of Jonah! For flesh and blood has not revealed this to you, but my Father in heaven" (Matt 16:17). This, of course, throws the rebuke into greater dialectical relief, particularly in light of Barth's insistence that the *identity* of Jesus as "the Christ, the Son of the Living God" is the normative viewpoint for all biblical interpretation, indeed, for all general interpretation as well! Setting one's mind on human things is directly and even satanically contrary to the divine revelation that is absolutely normative for interpretation and Christian proclamation. The appeal to Matthew, however, is unnecessary, as the rebuke itself is thoroughly dialectical, clearly qualifying the destiny of the Son of Man as "divine." With respect to Jesus' muted response to Peter's preceding confession, Mark simply emphasizes the dialectical aspect of "hiddenness." Either way, as with the debate in Mark 3 above, the crucial issue for preaching is the ability to discern the spirits.

Another important episode in which the "infinite qualitative difference" figures prominently is in Jesus' discourse with the rich young man (Mark 10:17–31). Here Jesus presents the tensions between the horizontal and the vertical movements, so to speak, in conversation with the young man. First, he sets God apart as the only good, saying: all that is not God is not good. Notice, he does *not* deny his own divinity here, does *not* deny that he himself is God, but he simply asks, "Why do you call me good? No one is good but God alone" (10:18). The proper response, in light of Peter's confession, *would* be, "But you are the Christ, the Son of the Living God!" The young man, however, is not as ready to recognize the divinity of Jesus, or at least, is not as close as that delightful scribe whom Jesus declares is "not far from the kingdom of God" (12:34). Instead, Jesus lays the horizontal, neighborly ethic before him in the form of the fifth through the tenth commandments (10:19). These the young man claims to have fulfilled, and Jesus, *graciously*, does not contradict him. Rather, he presents him with the ideal requirement, which is only revealed in light of the vertical diastasis: "You lack one thing; go, sell what you own, and give the money to the poor, and you will have treasure in heaven; then come, follow me" (10:21; but see also Matt 19:21, where Jesus says, "If you wish to be perfect ...").

The critical distinction emerges again with utmost clarity in the subsequent discussion with the disciples (Mark 10:24–31). There Jesus sets up an utterly "impossible" dialectic. "It is easier for a camel to go through the eye of a needle than for someone who is rich to enter the kingdom of God" (10:25). Read dialectically, this eye of the needle is not the name of an actual gate through which Jerusalem's camels had to wriggle. Neither is the camel a "thick rope" which had to be stuffed through a conventional sewing needle's eye. These belong to the category of quantitative analogy, not qualitative dialectic. Understood dialectically, it is a real, full-sized camel and an extra-fine needle. The contrast must not be mitigated in any way, since the very point is the impossibility for mortals to either perform or even imagine the task. "For mortals it is impossible, but not for God; for God all things are possible" (10:27). Peter again provides the opening for further elaboration, which is stated in terms of temporality and eternity, in terms of the promise that the followers of the Word (to borrow the Johannine reference) will "receive a hundredfold now in this age" and "in the age to come eternal life" (10:29–30).

To some extent, Jesus' debate with the Sadducees (Mark 12:12–17) may be best understood according to the *analogia fidei*. The Sadducees, who "say there is no resurrection," put Jesus on the spot regarding a doctrine in which they themselves do not believe. Their attitude is precisely the disbelief, or unfaith, that renders one an outsider. Preachers should note, however, that again the issue at stake in this debate is scriptural interpretation. What is telling here is that Jesus' retort not only (twice) pronounces the skeptical interpreters "wrong," he also attributes their error to their biblical illiteracy *coupled with* their lack of knowledge, perception, or discernment (*me eidotes*; Lat. *nescire*) of the power of God. "Is not this the reason you are wrong, that you know neither the scriptures nor the power of God?" (12:24) Jesus uses a parallelism to directly associate revelation through scripture with divine assistance! Furthermore, he affirms the resurrection of the dead by contrasting marriage, which belongs to temporal human existence, with eternal life, where the raised "are like angels in heaven" (12:25). "He is God not of the dead, but of the living; you are quite wrong" (12:27). In short, according to a dialectical reading, dead no longer means dead, since the patriarchs, Abraham, Isaac, and Jacob, are very much alive before the living God (12:26). In contrast to Buttrick's hermeneutical foreclosure on the possibility of learning anything of the afterlife from the parables, a dialectical reading of this text offers just such a possibility. How else shall mortals learn that the dead are not dead?

One other saying of Jesus must be mentioned which clearly demonstrates the importance of dialectical interpretation and the possibility of "insider" understanding.

> While Jesus was teaching in the temple, he said, "How can the scribes say that the Messiah is the son of David? David himself, by the Holy Spirit, declared, 'The Lord said to my Lord, "Sit at my right hand, until I put your enemies under your feet."' David himself calls him Lord; so how can he be his son?" (12:35–37)

Here Jesus again places scribal interpretation under scrutiny. He does not deny the truth of their teaching that the Messiah *is* the Son of David, but he simply poses the epistemological question: "How do they know?" Further, he establishes the seemingly contradictory point, that the Messiah is David's "Lord," by sealing it with the assurance that David was speaking with the authority of the Holy Spirit when he penned this particular psalm and the psalms generally. In fact, there is nothing to prevent us from interpreting Jesus as affirming the inspiration of scripture in the broadest (canonical) sense. Again, however, "insider" Christian tradition knows the answer to the riddle: that Jesus is not only the human heir to David, but the divine Son of God. This discernment is only possible, however, in terms of the vertical dialectic. The hermeneutic of a horizontally emerging new social reality cannot make heads or tails of this saying.

Students will surely easily identify other sayings of Jesus that highlight their dialectical content. Two others are worthy of brief mention. First, to return for a moment to the debate of 11:27—12:12 in which we find the parable of the wicked tenants, we should note that Jesus interprets the parable himself with a diastatic statement that stands outside the parable proper. "Have you not read this scripture: 'The stone that the builders rejected has become the cornerstone; this was the Lord's doing, and it is amazing in our eyes'?" (12:10–11). Here such a dialectical reading reveals that, not only did Jesus tell "this parable against" (12:12) the "builders," he also told it about himself as the rejected "cornerstone," the murdered son, though *without* testifying to himself directly. Second, Jesus' reply in his debate with "some Pharisees and Herodians" over the issues of taxation is thoroughly diastatic. "Give to the emperor the things that are the emperor's, and to God the things that are God's" (12:17).

The following is a partial list of other passages that may arise:

2:17	"Those who are well have no need of a physician, but those who are sick; I have come to call not the righteous but sinners."
2:18–22	*Statements about the bridegroom, his guests, and fasting.*
2:25–28	*Picking grain on the Sabbath and the Son of Man as Lord of the Sabbath.*
8:14–21	*Warnings against the yeast of the Pharisees.*
9:31	*Prophecy of the destiny of the Son of Man who is to be* "betrayed into human hands, and they will kill him, and three days after being killed, he will rise again."
9:33–37	*The argument on the way to Capernaum.* "Whoever wants to be first must be last of all and servant of all."
9:42–50	*Admonitions to remove stumbling blocks and temptations to sin.*
10:1–12	*The debate concerning divorce:* "what God has joined together, let no one separate."
10:35–45	*The request of James and John.*
11:17	*The cleansing of the temple.* "Is it not written, 'My house shall be called a house of prayer for all the nations'? But you have made it a den of robbers."
12:43–44	*The widow gives out of her poverty.*
13:11	*Relying on the Holy Spirit to give testimony under persecution.*
14:3–9	*The woman with the alabaster jar.* "For you always have the poor with you, and you can show kindness to them whenever you wish; but you will not always have me."
14:18–25	*The Institution of the Lord's Supper.* "Truly I tell you, I will never again drink of the fruit of the vine until that day when I drink it new in the kingdom of God."
14:27	*Peter's denial is foretold.* "You will all become deserters; for it is written, 'I will strike the shepherd, and the sheep will be scattered.'"

14:36–38	*The temptation in the Garden of Gethsemane.* "Abba, Father, for you all things are possible; remove this cup from me; yet, not what I want, but what you want." *Jesus' words to Peter.* "The spirit indeed is willing, but the flesh is weak."
14:48–49	*Jesus' words to the guards:* "Have you come out with swords and clubs to arrest me as though I were a bandit? Day after day I was with you in the temple teaching, and you did not arrest me. But let the scriptures be fulfilled."
14:62	*Jesus' reply to the high priest.* "I am; and 'you will see the Son of Man seated at the right hand of the Power,' and 'coming with the clouds of heaven.'"

§3.3.4 THE *ANALOGIA FIDEI*: FAITH IS OF GOD, WHOSE WAYS ARE NOT OUR WAYS

The *analogia fidei* has been with us in the background throughout this essay. In this final section, we will endeavor to bring it to the foreground and simply flesh out Barth's understanding of the term. We recall McCormack's contention that this form of analogy must be understood as throughly dialectical. This is borne out in *DGD*, where Barth presupposes

> that reason and religion on the one side, and revelation and faith on the other, cannot be conjoined quantitatively, and are not therefore to be put on the same level and intertwined, but must be soberly kept apart dialectically as question and answer. Only then . . . can they be strictly brought together and related to one another, in an iron hinge which moves up and down, not in glue that is meant to put them on a single surface. Then we shall no longer finish up with those barren quantitative distinctions and debates about reason and revelation, faith and knowledge, etc., which the modern age has made into the veritable passion story of theology. No, when God reveals himself, this means that God himself, known *and* making known, speaking *and* hearing, is present on the stage, and no matter whether we call this revelation or faith, it is an event with which what we do in our own sphere may well be in analogy but cannot be in continuity, as though our thinking and feeling were a kind of outflow or continuation of revelation . . .[125]

125. Barth, *DGD*, 94; emphasis mine.

For Barth, God is, in fact, "knowable" by the human, but only as revelation is "brought into effect" by God, by whom alone, "wholly and utterly," the human exists "as a believer."[126] Arvin Vos states it idiomatically. "A word applied to creature and then to God has similarity in its meaning, partial correspondence and agreement, only because it has been chosen by God."[127] Perhaps the most concise test of the *analogia fidei*, however, is stated in *CD* II.1, under the paragraph entitled, "The Being of God as the One Who Loves in Freedom" (§28).

> The legitimacy of every theory concerning the relationship of God and man or God and the world can be tested by considering whether it can be understood also as an interpretation of the relationship and fellowship created and sustained in Jesus Christ. Is it capable of adaptation to the fundamental insights of the Church concerning the person and work of Jesus Christ— the *analogia fidei*? . . . There are strictly speaking no Christian themes independent of Christology, and the Church must insist on this in its message to the world.[128]

It is in light of this clarification of the *analogia fidei* that we will, in this final section, simply gather, without elaboration, those sayings in which *pistis* [faith, belief, trust] dialectically signals the promise of revelation. In many cases, students of preaching generally will be able to locate many of these sayings with a simple word search. Following is a partial list of the texts that will likely arise:

1:14–15	*Jesus announces the coming of the kingdom and begins his Galilean ministry.* "The time is fulfilled, and the kingdom of God has come near; repent, and believe in the good news."
2:5	*Jesus heals a paralytic.* "When Jesus saw their faith, he said to the paralytic, 'Son, your sins are forgiven.'"
4:35–41	*Jesus calms a storm at sea.*
5:21–43	*Faith figures decisively in the healing of both a woman with a hemorrhage and Jairus' daughter.*

---

126. Barth, *CD* 1/1:229–47.

127. Arvin Vos, "Analogy," 6–7.

128. Barth, *CD* 2/1:320.

9:14–28	*Faith and prayer are instrumental in the healing of a mute boy with an unclean spirit.*[129]
10:46–52	*Jesus heals Blind Bartimaeus, saying:* "Go; your faith has made you well."
11:22–25	*Peter is amazed at the withered fig tree which Jesus had cursed. Jesus replies:* "Have faith in God. Truly I tell you, if you say to this mountain, 'Be taken up and thrown into the sea,' and if you do not doubt in your heart, but believe that what you say will come to pass, it will be done for you. So I tell you, whatever you ask for in prayer, believe that you have received it, and it will be yours. Whenever you stand praying, forgive, if you have anything against anyone; so that your Father in heaven may also forgive you your trespasses."
13:21–23	*Apocalyptic warnings against believing in false messiahs, after which Jesus assures the disciples,* "But be alert; I have already told you everything."
16:11–17	[*The longer ending of Mark, in which*] *the risen Jesus* "upbraided (the eleven) for their lack of faith and stubbornness, because they had not believed those who saw him after he had risen." *The disciples are told,* "The one who believes and is baptized will be saved; but the one who does not believe will be condemned."

Finally, one particular passage, which is not a saying of Jesus, is nevertheless of some interest in light of Barth's Christological definition of the *analogia fidei.*

| 15:32 | *The jeering of the crowd illustrates the satanic attempt to redefine* pistis *in terms of self-concern and self-preservation, i.e., Jesus' coming down from the cross:* "Let the Messiah, the King of Israel, come down from the cross now, so that we may see and believe." |

Conclusion

Barth was one theologian who held that theorizing about interpretation apart from actually doing it was a fruitless exercise. In the words of his biographer, Eberhard Busch, Barth "refused to involve himself in a discussion which was purely about the method of exegesis and was

---

129. Barth upholds the cry of the boy's father (Mark 9:24) as indicating his "biblical attitude" which "is most simple and naive and direct: 'I believe, Lord, help thou my unbelief.'" *DGD*, 290.

not involved in the exegesis of particular texts. He thought that 'herme-neutics cannot be an independent topic of conversation; its problems can only be tackled and answered in countless acts of interpretation."[130] At the risk of exhausting the reader with my own "countless acts of interpretation," I have not only tried to supply some clarification with regard to the dialectical character of Barth's theology and responded to two recent critics of his interpretive and homiletical views, I have also attempted to appropriate Barth's enduring dialectic (termed by Bruce McCormack as *diastasis*) for homiletical pedagogy and offered a ratio-nale for its use by identifying its ubiquitous operation in the speeches of Jesus in the Gospel of Mark.

In my view, this requires a leap away from the formalistic approach advocated by the New Homiletic, a leap that indeed (1) aims *beyond* the apparent relevance of preaching ethics, (2) ventures a thoroughly dialectical and Christologically-tested understanding of the content of scripture, and (3) awakens our sensibilities to the need to develop with full intentionality a pneumatic doctrine of homiletical interpretation that hermeneutics itself has for too long forestalled and obstructed. Narrative preaching has, to a considerable extent, misdirected its ener-gies toward a hermeneutical emphasis on parable in an effort to emulate Jesus' method of preaching. We have seen, however, that when the fo-cus is shifted to a dialectical reading of the fuller content of Jesus' say-ings, the *diastasis* that emerges with a remarkable consistency may be paraphrased, "God's ways are not our ways" (Isa 55:8–9). Further, while fixation on parable tends to obscure interpretation, a rigorous adher-ence to the presupposition of the infinite qualitative difference between the Creator and the creature, between the eternal and the temporal, is disclosive precisely because it positions the interpreter according to the universals of the human condition (e.g., mortality, sin, etc.), not merely in relation to other socio-cultural conditions (as in general anthropol-ogy), but strictly (as per theological anthropology) with respect to God, and it is in this posture alone that one can recognize and receive the revealed God-man for what, for who, and for whom he is: the hidden One who alone sovereignly discloses himself, that is, *by* faith, *to* faith, *for* faith. The assertion that "God's ways are not human ways," I contend, is not "merely" a confession of faith, but is the presupposed content

130. Busch, *Karl Barth*, 349.

formulation that must be upheld as *the first guiding interpretive rule for Christian preaching, evangelism, education, mission,* and *nurture.* It is nothing short of *the universal "context" for Christian preaching and ministry, the context that transcends the regnant paradigms of anthropological sophism and hermeneutical contextualism, the everywhere identifiable status quo into which the gospel must be proclaimed.* It is rooted in the first Christian anthropological assertion of humanity's condition in temporality, namely, that we labor under the burden of sin and that we are in need of forgiveness, grace, regeneration, transformation, sanctification, and revelation, needs that we can in no way supply for ourselves. "Faith itself, obedient faith, but faith, and in the last resort obedient faith alone, is the activity which is demanded of us as members of the Church, the exercise of the *freedom* which is granted to us *under* the Word."[131]

---

131. Barth, *CD* 1/2:740; emphasis mine.

2

Contemporaneity in the Dock

A Critical Comparison of Kierkegaard's Christo-Pneumatology and Gadamer's Meta-critical Hermeneutics

Introduction

IN THE FOREGOING CHAPTER, I MADE MUCH (!?) OF THE KIERKE-gaardian/Barthian category of "the infinite qualitative difference" between the divine and the human, between eternity and temporality. It is perhaps helpful to recall, however, that when Kierkegaard introduced this qualitative aspect of his dialectic, he was *not* advocating for an infinite qualitative *distance*. In fact, his Christology is such that the God-man bears this difference in his two natures with no distinguishable distance per se, even though his two natures remain unconfused and qualitatively distinct. Thus, although the *diastasis* under consideration is best understood in terms of a qualitative distinction between dimensions, for lack of a better term, the spatial dimensions are, nevertheless, not what is meant. To borrow from Cartesian thought for a moment, let us assume that the spatial categories of length, width, and depth represent the first three dimensions, and time the fourth dimension. This understanding of the multi-dimensionality of space and time is widely held, but at this point a clear lack of consensus arises as to the nature of the fifth dimension. From a Kierkegaardian perspective, however, the nature of *the moment*, wherein eternity intersects temporality at a right angle, so to speak, suggests that nothing less than eternity itself, the realm of faith and spirit, constitutes a fifth dimension. This is neither the place to enter into speculation regarding any further levels of dimensionality or multi-dimensionality, nor is it my intention to defend a quasi-Cartesian structure to the universe, but it is well to recall that the nature of the *diastasis* which we have been considering lies beyond all spatial restrictions, and further, involves a leap beyond any merely linear notion of temporality and history. This is not to say that in dealing with Kierkegaard's view of contemporaneity we will be able to avoid the use of spatial metaphors, but it is to say that the nexus under consideration in the dialectic of contemporaneity is at the point where mundane temporality is suspended and the God-man becomes every bit as real and present (not from the past, but from eternity) to the earthly creature as he was to the first apostles who touched and bore witness to his resurrected body. This will be important to bear in mind as we seek to distinguish between Kierkegaard's understanding of contemporaneity and that of Hans-Georg Gadamer, who attempted to put it to a different use entirely.

In his monumental *Truth and Method*, Gadamer mentions Kierkegaard relatively infrequently. Nevertheless, in its pages, one finds occasional attempts at appropriation from, and expressions of appreciation for, Kierkegaard, as well as points of departure from him.[1] Foremost among these features, involving both appropriation and departure, is the matter of contemporaneity. Here, I will offer only the most concise synopsis of *Truth and Method*, briefly noting points of affinity and discontinuity with Kierkegaard along the way, so as to give primary attention to Gadamer's construal of contemporaneity. I will conclude by commenting on the implications of this category for discernment and proclamation, and more specifically, on the importance of giving it its proper Christo-pneumatic significance and setting it apart radically from hermeneutics per se.

§1. A Brief Summary of *Truth and Method*

Gadamer was a student of Heidegger and a leading modern exponent of hermeneutics.[2] In *Truth and Method,* he tries to clarify the *phenomenon*

---

1. For an appreciative assessment of Gadamer's reception of Kierkegaard, particularly on their shared penchant for paradox, see Dunning, "Paradoxes in Interpretation," 125–41.

2. For a good general summaries of Gadamer's thought, see Inwood, "Gadamer, Hans-Georg," 303; Jeanrond, *Theological Hermeneutics*, 64–70; and Thiselton, *New Horizons*, 313–43.

of understanding, by contrasting understanding [*Verstehen*] as a human attitude[3] with the explanatory function [*Erklären*] of the *natural sciences*. Gadamer took issue with the way in which his hermeneutical forebear, Wilhelm Dilthey, had sharply and idealistically assigned *understanding* to *the humanities* and *explanation* to the *natural sciences*. For Gadamer, understanding is performed *not only* by *natural* scientists but also by *non*-scientists and *cultural* scientists. Understanding is able to consider as its object: speech, texts, people, works of art, and historical events. Whereas early hermeneuts attempted to refine a methodology for the proper interpretation of these entities, Gadamer contested that they failed to regard their own understanding as an object of their consideration, that their own interpretations were historically conditioned.[4] Indeed, his proposal is radically anti-methodological.[5] Per Gadamer, historical and cultural situation involves a particular pre-understanding or "horizon." Understanding involves an interplay between past and present, and thus, finally, a "fusion of horizons." Since all interpretations are historically conditioned, the best we can manage is "authentic" interpretation by making the best reflective use of the prejudices from which we inevitably begin.

In Part I of *Truth and Method*, Gadamer considers "the question of truth as it emerges in the experience [*Erlebnis*] of art." *Erlebnis* is something one *has* as an *esthetic experience*. Gadamer wants to "retrieve the question of artistic truth." He contends that the work of art has ontological importance. The category of *play* for Gadamer offers a clue to *ontological explanation* as it involves *total mediation* or *re-presentation*.[6] He states: "the play of art does not simply exhaust itself in momentary

---

3. Jeanrond, *Theological Hermeneutics*, 65–67.

4. Clearly there is something akin to Kierkegaard's anti-Hegelian polemic at work here, that is, to his complaint that the systematic thinker who starts from nothing tends to forget he exists.

5. For this reason, Jeanrond suggests a more fitting title to Gadamer's proposal would be "Truth *or* Method," since Gadamer "sees a radical conflict between his phenomenological approach to hermeneutics on the one hand and the host of methodological proposals for an adequate text-understanding on the other hand"; see Jeanrond, *Theological Hermeneutics*, 69. Thiselton states it still more emphatically: "Gadamer's work constitutes a full-scale attack on the role of method in hermeneutics"; see Thiselton, *New Horizons*, 313.

6. Gadamer contends that his terminology of "total mediation" is equivalent to or synonymous with Kierkegaard's description of successfully achieving the situation of contemporaneity; *TM*, 572–73.

transport, but has a claim to permanence and the permanence of a claim." By "permanence" I understand Gadamer to mean, that which is able to account for the enduring influence an artwork has over time. Further, by the word *claim* he means "something lasting," something that "can be enforced at any time. A claim exists against someone and must therefore be enforced against him. . . . A claim is the legal basis for an unspecified demand."

It is in this context that Gadamer explicitly mentions Kierkegaard's dialectical theology as the source for his thinking on the matter of contemporaneity, yet with the clear assumption that the theological or Christological sense given it by Kierkegaard is but a particular instance of its importance.[7] In doing so, Gadamer distinguishes, at least tentatively, between the claims of faith that pertain to preaching the gospel and legal claims, as well as the truth claims that may be attributed to a work of art. Thus, Kierkegaard's qualitative distinctions between the esthetic, the ethical, and the religious spheres of existence figure in Gadamer's thought *to a degree*, so to speak, with the result that he takes what is in some respects a relatively high view of authority and preaching.[8]

In Part II, Gadamer lists three necessary elements of a theory of hermeneutical experience. First, the historicity of understanding must be elevated to a hermeneutical problem. In other words, the hermeneutical circle involves prejudices as conditions of understanding. This requires, on the one hand, the rehabilitation of authority and tradition as legitimate "prejudices." But it also means that temporal distance bears hermeneutical significance, because history has a double effect/affect on

7. "In the theological reflection that began with Kierkegaard and which we call 'dialectical theology,' it is no accident that this concept [i.e. of a lasting 'claim'] has made possible a theological explanation of what Kierkegaard meant by contemporaneity." "The concept of contemporaneity, we know, stems from Kierkegaard, who gave it a particular theological stamp," *TM*, 127. Gadamer cites the fourth chapter "and elsewhere" of the Kierkegaard's pseudonymous *Philosophical Fragments*, but he is not specific. In other words, there is no clear indication that Gadamer has in mind here the later, more developed, and specifically Christological view of contemporaneity as we find it in, say, *Practice in Christianity*.

8. "The application of Lutheran theology is that the claim of faith began with the *proclamation of the gospel* and is *continually reinforced in preaching*. The words of the sermon perform this total mediation, which otherwise is the work of the religious rite—of the mass, for example. We shall see that in other ways too *the word is called on to mediate between past and present*, and that it therefore comes to play a leading role in the problem of hermeneutics," *TM*, 127; italics mine.

consciousness. "Consciousness of being effected by history is primarily consciousness of the hermeneutical situation. To acquire awareness of a situation is, however, always a task of peculiar difficulty. The very idea of a situation means that we are not standing outside it and hence are unable to have any objective knowledge of it."[9] Thus, as with certain other strains of hermeneutics that grant an exaggerated priority and finality to contextual considerations, there appears to be no possibility of the Archimedean point that Kierkegaard, especially in *Works of Love*,[10] clearly assigns to *faith*. The lack of such a point is, of course, perfectly true vis-à-vis any concrete and finite situation or context. "Every *finite present* has its limitations. We define the concept of 'situation' by saying that it represents a standpoint that limits the possibility of vision. Hence essential to the concept of situation is the concept of 'horizon.' The horizon is the range of vision that includes everything that can be seen from a particular vantage point."[11] Gadamer rightly insists that the process of *foregrounding* [*abheben*] requires a constant vigilance "against overhastily assimilating *the past* to our own expectations of meaning. Only then can we listen to tradition in a way that permits it to make its own meaning heard."[12]

The second element of Gadamer's theory of hermeneutical experience is the recovery of what he terms "the fundamental hermeneutical problem," namely, the problem of *application*. For Gadamer, the fusion of horizons is essentially a matter of application.[13] Here he credits *pietist hermeneutics*[14] with adding the third element of application (*applicandi*)

9. *TM*, 301.

10. Kierkegaard, *Works of Love*, 136, and n. 173.

11. *TM*, 302; italics mine.

12. *TM*, 305; italics mine.

13. "In the process of understanding a real fusion of horizons occurs—which means that as the historical horizon is projected, it is simultaneously superseded (or removed). To bring about this fusion in a regulated (or conscious) way is the task of what we called the historically effective consciousness. Although this task was obscured by aesthetic-historical positivism following on the heels of romantic hermeneutics, it is, in fact, the central problem of hermeneutics. It is the problem of *application,* which is to be found in all understanding," *TM*, 307.

14. *TM*, 307; Gadamer mentions, in particular, J. J. Rambach, *Institutiones Sacræ Hermeneuticæ*, ed. Morus (Jena: 1723). Elsewhere, however, hermeneutical theorists have shown far less appreciation for Rambach's pietism. Friedrich Lücke, e.g., in his 1838 edition of Schleiermacher's lectures on hermeneutics, also notes Rambach's addition of *application*, "which recent authors are unfortunately stressing once again."

to the early hermeneutical *subtilitas* (talents, as opposed to methods) of understanding (*intelligendi*) and interpretation (*explicandi*). Yet the Romantics recognized the inner unity of understanding and interpretation. They are not to be seen as sequential steps; on the contrary, "interpretation is the explicit form of understanding."[15] As Gadamer explains, the "inner fusion of understanding and interpretation led to the third element in the hermeneutical problem, *application*, becoming wholly excluded from any connection with hermeneutics. The edifying application of Scripture in Christian preaching, for example, now seemed very different from the historical and theological understanding of it."[16] Gadamer's solution is to go one better than Romantic hermeneutics and regard *understanding, interpretation*, and *application* "as comprising one unified process."[17] Gadamer denies that this is a return to Pietism's three separate "*subtleties*." Rather, he says: "The fact that *philological, legal*, and *theological* hermeneutics originally belonged closely together" is indicative of the "integral element of all understanding."[18]

The third element in Gadamer's hermeneutical theory is that the historically-effected consciousness must be evident in the priority given to questioning, for which Platonic dialectic/dialogue and the logic of question and answer may be taken as a model. "For Gadamer, Plato's most important contribution comes in his exposition of dialogue as a process in which truth 'arises' in the to-and-fro of questions and of conversation."[19]

In Part III, Gadamer attends to the ontological shift of hermeneutics to a thoroughgoing attention to language. He argues that language is not only the medium of a hermeneutic of experience; it is also the horizon of hermeneutical ontology. Language is the contextually-conditioned

---

See Schleiermacher, *Hermeneutics and Criticism*, xxxvii and 5. See also Ebeling, *Word and Faith*, 311–31. Ebeling's views have, of course, had enormous influence upon late twentieth century preaching. Thus we should not be surprised that Buttrick, e.g., has expressly denounced the very notion of "a so-called holy hermeneutic." See Buttrick, *Homiletic*, 274 and 277.

15. *TM*, 307.

16. Ibid., 308. By comparison, Christian Breuninger has argued that Kierkegaard's emphasis on application amounts to a "reformation of expository preaching." See Breuninger, "Kierkegaard's Reformation of Expository Preaching," 21–36.

17. *TM*, 308.

18. Ibid.

19. Thiselton, *New Horizons*, 321.

experience [*Erfahrung*] of the world, the on-going, integrative, formative, dialogical experience in and of history and tradition. Language is
not only the medium of experience, but also its speculative structure;
thus, Gadamer concludes that hermeneutics is a universal problem.

§2. A Critical Response to Gadamer

Interesting as it is, especially for its anti-methodologogical implications,
Gadamer's own view of contemporaneity, particularly as he applies it in
the sphere of esthetics, introduces a whole new set of problems. First,
Gadamer sees contemporaneity as a "task" facing the believer, whereas
Kierkegaard identified it with faith and located it in the presence of
Jesus Christ the God-man, not with art.[20] Admittedly, Kierkegaard
himself described contemporaneity in terms of *striving*, but specifically
striving *born of gratitude*, as a response to grace.[21] This might be what
Gadamer means by a "task *set* by contemporaneity," if we were able to
assume that for him contemporaneity were sufficiently freighted with
the Christological content of grace in the sphere of faith. But as we shall
see, there is reason to be concerned that Gadamer does not maintain
clearly enough either the distinction between faith and works, or a focus
that coheres sufficiently with his appeals to Christological analogues.

Second, in order to make his case for truth in the esthetic experience of *Erlebnis*, Gadamer must separate the truth claims of art via
contemporaneity, not only from the theological "stamp" given it by
Kierkegaard, thus presumably placing it at some remove from the

20. Gadamer's explanation is otherwise sound: "For Kierkegaard, 'contemporaneity'
does not mean 'existing at the same time.' Rather, it names the task that confronts the
believer: to bring together two moments that are not concurrent, namely one's own
present and the redeeming Christ, and yet so totally to mediate them that the latter is
experienced and taken seriously as present (and not as something in a distant past).
The simultaneity of aesthetic consciousness, by contrast, is just the opposite of this and
indeed is based on covering up and concealing the task set by contemporaneity." But
elsewhere the matter is stated rather meritoriously: "contemporaneity is not a mode of
givenness in consciousness, but a task for consciousness and an achievement that is
demanded of it." *TM*, 127.

21. Dunning also notes with some confusion Gadamer's choice of the word "task."
"The reference to the fourth chapter 'and elsewhere' in (*Philosophical Fragments*) is so
vague that it is hard to know just where Gadamer got the idea of contemporaneity as
a task. In (*Philosophical Fragments*) what we find is less a discussion of 'task' than a
sustained critique of the notion of 'immediate contemporaneity.'" Dunning, "Paradoxes
in Interpretation," 140 n. 3.

God-relation, but also from what he calls "the simultaneity of aesthetic consciousness."

> In any case, *"contemporaneity"* belongs to the being of the work of art. It constitutes the essence of "being present." This is *not* the *simultaneity* of *aesthetic consciousness*, for that simply means that several objects of aesthetic experience (*Erlebnis*) are held in consciousness at the same time . . . "Contemporaneity," on the other hand, means that in its presentation this particular thing that presents itself to us achieves full presence, however remote its origin may be. . . . It consists in holding on to the thing in such a way that it becomes "contemporaneous," which is to say, however, that all mediation is superseded in total presence.[22]

One gets the impression that, while Gadamer is aware of the distinction between Kierkegaard's existential spheres (i.e., he goes to great lengths to avoid the lapse into mere esthetics),[23] he is not altogether successful in maintaining them, at least not according to Kierkegaard's qualitative strictures. Clearly, he does aim to avoid "the destructive consequences of subjectivism and the . . . self-annihilating of aesthetic immediacy," which came under Kierkegaard's negative critique.[24] What is not at all clear is how, according to Gadamer's understanding of contemporaneity, the remote, yet fully present "thing," if it is *not* the God-man, is to be differentiated from, say, a graven image or an idol. One would expect Gadamer to have taken the question, pious as it sounds, more seriously, for (1) he himself shows certain pietistic sympathies, (2) he expresses concern about "Hegel's concept of a 'religion of art,'"[25] and (3) he nevertheless correlates his claims for artistic truth to Christian worship and preaching.[26] In light of this, preaching must ask in earnest,

---

22. *TM*, 127; italics mine; see also 572–73, where Gadamer argues that the distinction is Kierkegaardian. It seems clear, however, that Gadamer confuses the search for truth in the esthetic sphere with what I believe Kierkegaard would describe as the "esthetic validity" of truth in the higher spheres, and most unambiguously, in the sphere of Christian faith. In short, according to Kierkegaard's "stages on life's way," the esthetic does re-emerge in the higher spheres, but not as a sphere or a *telos* unto itself. Rather, it reemerges as a secondary and derivative property within the higher spheres.

23. See esp. *TM*, 95–96.

24. Ibid., 95.

25. Ibid., 573.

26. "Contemporaneity in this [i.e., Christological] sense is found especially in religious rituals and in the proclamation of the Word in preaching. Here 'being present'

if contemporaneity is not to be understood Christo-pneumatically (specifically vis-à-vis the risen Christ and the Holy Spirit), but merely analogically and hermeneutically, *what* precisely is "the being of the artwork" that is achieving full presence? If the God-man is not the agent of this "total mediation," then how is Gadamer's correlation to worship warranted in such a way that avoids turning the experience of art into misdirected worship, or adoration of the wrong "thing"?[27] It is a question that Gadamer never adequately addresses.[28]

My third concern is that the "total mediation" of "the being of the artwork itself" requires contemporaneity at all. If the artwork itself is fully present, whence the temporal distance and the need for bridging it? In fact it does appear that, for Gadamer, it is a matter strictly of *temporal* distance, that his dialectic is one that presupposes the permanence and lasting endurance, i.e., *through* time, of the truth content of works of art, but not (as for Kierkegaard) eternity per se. Thus, as with Gadamer's elevation of historicity (see below), the eternal-temporal qualification, and the qualitative nature of Kierkegaard's dialectic between the esthetic and the sphere of Christian faith (in which the God-man is both "the object of faith" as well as faith's Sovereign Subject), have not been maintained strictly enough, since the work of art is now the object of consideration

---

means genuine participation in the redemptive event itself. No one can doubt that aesthetic differentiation—attending to how 'beautiful' the ceremony was or how 'well preached' the sermon—is out of place, given the kind of claim that is made on us. *Now, I maintain that the same thing is basically true when we experience art. Here too the mediation must be thought of as total.* Neither the being that the creating artist is for himself . . . nor that of whoever is performing the work, nor that of the spectator watching the play, has any legitimacy of its own in the face of the being of the artwork itself." Ibid., 128.

27. In the following passage, e.g., Gadamer uses the biblical term for the presence, or the second coming, of Christ: *parousia*. Absent any clear statement, however, of the infinite qualitative difference between Christ and, say, a very fine painting, we are left to wonder how it is that the latter is to be accorded the godlike power to *achieve* "absolute presence" and establish, or re-establish, the self: "Just as the ontological mode of aesthetic being is marked by *parousia*, absolute presence, and just as an artwork is nevertheless self-identical in every moment where it achieves such a presence, so also the absolute moment in which a spectator stands is both one of self-forgetfulness and of mediation with himself. What rends him from himself at the same time gives him back the whole of his being." Ibid., 128.

28. Thus, we concur with Joel Weinsheimer's description of Gadamer's post-modern thrust as "relativism with a vengeance . . . absolute relativism." Cited in Thiselton, *New Horizons*, 314.

in Gadamer's dialectic of contemporaneity. In other words, no "lasting" or "permanent" work of art is really up to the task of fulfilling the role of *eternity* in the dialectical relation of contemporaneity.

From the perspective of Kierkegaard's qualitative dialectic, however, Gadamer's statement of the hermeneutical problem is dominated by his concern for the limited perspective granted by any finite situation, to the extent that the problem for him is strictly one of not only spatial, but temporal distance, of the "past" of tradition and the "present" which is always in flux. So it is with Gadamer's popular concept of the fusion of horizons, which renders his dialectic a flat, quantitative comparison *within* temporality. On the one hand, he insists: "a hermeneutical situation is determined by the prejudices we bring with us. They constitute . . . the horizon of a particular present, for they represent that beyond which it is impossible to see." On the other hand, the present situation that is characterized by ever-changing prejudices, does not constitute a fixed horizon, or a "fixed set of opinions and valuations;" rather, it is

> continually in the process of being formed because we are continually having to test all our prejudices. An important part of this testing occurs in encountering the past and in understanding the tradition from which we come. Hence the horizon of the present cannot be formed without the past. There is no more an isolated horizon of the present in itself than there are historical horizons which have to be acquired. Rather, understanding is always the fusion of these horizons supposedly existing in themselves. . . . In a tradition this process of fusion is continually ongoing . . .[29]

In other words, temporal change and temporal distance together constitute the totality of the problem. At no point does Gadamer allow the qualitatively different dimension of eternity, the Archimedean point of the "expectancy of faith,"[30] or faith that is essentially contrary to and incommensurate with sight (2 Cor 5:7; Heb 11:1), to factor among the "prejudices" which he seeks to legitimate. The elevation of temporality in the form of "the historicity of understanding" obscures the eternal altogether and overtakes the possibility of a properly qualitative dialectic.[31]

29. *TM*, 306.

30. The theme of Kierkegaard's first published discourse; see *Eighteen Upbuilding Discourses*, 7–29.

31. It is worth recalling that this is not the way in which Climacus stated the problem in *Philosophical Fragments*, where it is not so much a matter of the temporal distance

In sum, Gadamer's description of the dialectical tension involved in the hermeneutical problem is consistently stated in temporal terms.[32]

Fourth, Gadamer's appeal to integration as the *sole* distinction between his own theory of hermeneutical experience and that of pietism, however, is not convincing. Despite the correctness of his statement that neither law nor gospel exist in order to be understood as merely historical documents, nevertheless, his argument for the necessarily effective application of the law and the gospel[33]—a necessity which Kierkegaard certainly upholds by defining Christianity in terms of an "existence-communication" and "striving" in imitation of Christ—becomes the basis of Gadamer's frequent comparative association between *legal* and *theological* hermeneutics:

> *Hermeneutics* in the sphere of philology and the historical sciences is not 'knowledge as domination'—i.e., an appropriation as taking possession; rather, it *consists in subordinating ourselves to the text's claim to dominate our minds. Of this,* however, *legal and theological hermeneutics are the true model. To interpret the law's will or the promises of God is clearly not a form of domination but of service.* They are interpretations—which includes application - in the service of what is considered valid. Our thesis is that historical hermeneutics too has a task of application to

---

between the past historical event and the contemporary, finite situation of the believer, but that a "historical point of departure" may be taken "for an eternal consciousness," and that "an eternal happiness" may be "built on historical knowledge." See Kierkegaard, *Philosophical Fragments*, 1.

32. "Every encounter with tradition that takes place within historical consciousness involves the experience of a tension between the text and the present. The hermeneutic task consists in not covering up this tension by attempting a naive assimilation of the two but in consciously bringing it out. This is why it is part of the hermeneutic approach to project a historical horizon that is different from the horizon of the present. Historical consciousness is aware of its own otherness and hence foregrounds the horizons of the past from its own. On the other hand, it is itself . . . only something superimposed upon continuing tradition, and hence it immediately recombines with what it has foregrounded itself from in order to become one with itself again in the unity of the historical horizon that it thus acquires. / Projecting a historical horizon, then, is only one phase in the process of understanding; it does not become solidified into the self-alienation of a past consciousness, but is overtaken by our own present horizon of understanding." *TM*, 306–7.

33. "This implies that the text, *whether legal or gospel*, if it is to be understood properly—i.e., according to the claim it makes, must be understood at every moment, in every concrete situation, in a new and different way. Understanding here is always application." Ibid., 309; italics mine.

perform, because it too serves applicable meaning, in that it explicitly and consciously bridges the temporal distance that separates the interpreter from the text and overcomes the alienation of meaning that the text has undergone.[34]

Here we find the very sense of subjectivity that is also detectable in Kierkegaard's highly qualified view of the truth-relation, that is, subjectivity as subordinating oneself to Christ as the Truth (John 14:6),[35] except that with Gadamer, this self-subordination throws off all qualifications. Not only do we find little distinction between law and gospel here, but every other text and object of historical interest is now elevated to the same level, each one equally eligible to register a permanent claim and receive the service and devotion of the self.[36] Thus, for Gadamer, understanding is essentially (1) historical, and therefore temporal at every point, and (2) in contrast to a method, it is an event of self-subordination or voluntary subjection to just about any temporal game or object that "masters the players" and "holds the players in its spell."[37]

But is it really fair to say that Gadamer fails to distinguish between legal and theological interpretation? In one key passage, for instance, he draws some requisite and helpful distinctions, and in a way that suggests a properly high view of scriptural authority and the unchanging content of Christian proclamation, even as he allows this content to dissolve into concern for "interpreting *a* valid truth."[38] Nevertheless,

---

34. Ibid., 311; italics mine.

35. See Slemmons, "Penitential Homiletic," 183–232.

36. "In reality then, legal hermeneutics is no special case but is, on the contrary, capable of restoring the hermeneutical problem to its full breadth and so re-establishing the former unity of hermeneutics, in which jurist and theologian meet the philologist." *TM*, 328.

37. Ibid., 106. This latter qualification is supposedly rendered benign, stripped of the possibility of domination, by virtue of Gadamer's assumption of goodwill on the part of the player/observer, and his exclusive focus on a "happy outcome." Clearly not everyone is convinced by Gadamer's optimism, but an evaluation of the critiques of Paul Ricoeur, Jürgen Habermas, et al., are beyond our present scope.

38. Ibid., 330–31; italics mine. Regarding *theological hermeneutics*, "as developed by Protestant theology," Gadamer writes, "Here there is a genuine parallel to legal hermeneutics, for here too dogmatics cannot claim any primacy. The proclamation is genuinely concretized in preaching, as is the legal order in judgment. But there is still a big difference between them. Unlike a legal verdict, preaching is not a creative supplement to the text it is interpreting. Hence the gospel acquires no new content in being preached that could be compared with the power of the judge's verdict to supplement

there does appear a critical departure from Kierkegaard on the matter of Gadamer's claim that "the *primary* thing is application."

> As a Protestant art of interpreting scripture, modern herme-
> neutics is clearly related in a polemical way to the dogmatic
> tradition of the Catholic church. It has itself a dogmatic denom-
> inational significance. This does not mean that such theological
> hermeneutics is dogmatically predisposed, so that it reads out
> of the text what it has put into it. Rather, it really risks itself.
> But it assumes that the word of Scripture addresses us and that
> *only* the person who *allows* himself to be addressed—*whether
> he believes or doubts* - understands. Hence the *primary* thing is
> application.[39]

Certainly Kierkegaard would be the last to diminish or deny the risk. The point of divergence here is that for Gadamer the reader/ listener must allow himself to be addressed, while for Kierkegaard, whether one allows it or not, one will either believe or take offense. The difference is subtle, but Gadamer makes even doubt contingent on the hearer's (passive) volition, that is, he permits a neutral ground of non-responsiveness, while for Kierkegaard, the response of faith or offense will happen regardless of one's "allowance." The possibility of offense is *inescapable*. Given this departure, it is not surprising then that Gadamer elevates application to a primary status, while Kierkegaard, despite his insistence on the application of imitation, never loses sight of the fact that the works of love are the "minor premise" of Christianity. Instead of employing Kierkegaard's qualitative antithesis of sin and faith,[40] Gadamer remains in the quantitative realm in which there are only ever degrees of faith and doubt. To Gadamer's credit, he does recognize the unchanging and salvific content of the gospel proclamation in a way

---

the law. It is not the case that the gospel of salvation becomes more clearly determined only through the preacher's thoughts. As a preacher, he does not speak before the com-munity with the same dogmatic authority that a judge does. Certainly preaching too is concerned with interpreting a valid truth, but this truth is proclamation; and whether it is successful or not is not decided by the ideas of the preacher, but by the power of the word itself, which can call men to repentance even though the sermon is a bad one. The proclamation cannot be detached from its fulfillment. The dogmatic establishment of pure doctrine is a secondary matter. Scripture is the word of God, and that means that it has absolute priority over the doctrine of those who interpret it. / Interpretation should never overlook this. Even as the scholarly interpretation of the theologian, it must never forget that Scripture is the divine proclamation of salvation."

39. Ibid., 332; italics mine.

40. Kierkegaard, *Sickness Unto Death*, 82, 105, and 124–31; see also Rom 14:23.

that postmodern hermeneutics generally does not. But he does not allow this content, specifically the presupposition of sin and the unavoidable possibility of offense (apart from which the gospel of salvation is meaningless and unnecessary), to inform scriptural interpretation or set it apart from general hermeneutics in any significant way. Whether the form of hermeneutics is legal, theological, philosophical, historical, or literary, application remains the "special activity of the reader and interpreter."[41] While we can certainly insist, with Gadamer, "neither the jurist nor the theologian regards the work of application as making free with the text;"[42] nevertheless, there appears no evidence here, as in Kierkegaard, that even the appropriation of the major premise of Christianity requires the assistance of the Holy Spirit.[43]

Concerning the dialectical element of Platonic questioning, Gadamer certainly shows some affinity with Kierkegaard's penchant for the Socratic. Nevertheless, this correspondence requires the following qualification, namely, that (1) Socratic indirection constitutes the minor—not (as is commonly held) the major—thrust in Kierkegaard's writings,[44] and that (2) the strictly temporal nature of Gadamer's dialectic is no substitute for the qualitative dialectic of contemporaneity in Kierkegaard. In his consideration of Gadamer's and Kierkegaard's shared affinity for the paradoxical, Stephen N. Dunning character-

41. *TM*, 332–33.

42. Ibid., 332.

43. "The Spirit brings faith, the faith—that is, faith in the strictest sense of the word, this gift of the Holy Spirit—only after death has come in between. We human beings are not very precise with words; we often talk about faith when in the strictly Christian sense it is not faith. According to the divergence of natural endowments, we are born with a stronger or weaker immediacy; the stronger, the more vigorous [*livskraftig*] it is, the longer it can hold out against resistance. And this endurance, this healthy [*livsfrisk*] confidence in oneself, in the world, in mankind, and, along with all this, in God, we call faith. But in the stricter Christian understanding it is not faith. Faith is against understanding; faith is on the other side of death. And when you died or died to yourself, to the world, then you also died to all immediacy in yourself, also to your understanding. It is when all confidence in yourself or in human support, and also in God in an immediate way, is extinct, when every probability is extinct, when it is dark as on a dark night—it is indeed death we are describing—then comes the life-giving Spirit and brings faith. This faith is stronger than the whole world; it has the power of eternity; it is the Spirit's gift from God, it is your victory over the world in which you more than conquer." Kierkegaard, *For Self-Examination/Judge for Yourself!*, 81–82.

44. I have treated this point at some length in my dissertation, "Penitential Homiletic."

izes the results of Gadamer's appeal to the conversational paradigm as follows: "Gadamer's hermeneutical conclusion—that questions have priority over answers—shows how fully his program involves the paradoxical sort of death and resurrection of knowledge that emerged in Kierkegaard's writings."[45] It would perhaps be more accurate in Kierkegaard's case, however, to speak of the death of knowledge (in the epistemic sense) and the "resurrection" (so to speak) of faith and love. For Gadamer, it may well be that knowledge, or understanding, undergoes a series of such noetic deaths and *recognitions*, but it is not at all clear that faith ever attains the status of Christianity's major premise, or that it is precisely faith that finally stands over against the lower existential stages or brings about the death of knowledge in order for faith itself to rise in its place.[46]

Having observed the absence of an eternal-temporal dialectic in *Truth and Method*, we must admit here that, by correlating language to the Christ, Gadamer does attempt to posit a paradoxical relation between the meeting of the infinite and the finite in the medium of language. The Incarnation functions as the decisive Christological locus for Gadamer's view of language, as it "prepares the way for a new philosophy of man," one that, in turn, "mediates in a new way between the mind of man in its finitude and the divine infinity. Here what we have called the hermeneutical experience finds its own, special ground."[47]

What is troubling about this view of language, however, is that while Gadamer does finally propose to account for the infinite element in what appears to be a qualitative dialectic, he attributes infinity not to the divine-human Logos, but to a linguistic analogue that bears no

45. Dunning, "Paradoxes in Interpretation," 135.

46. See *TM*, 573–74. In his "Afterword," Gadamer states that "the task of hermeneutical integration" "corresponds more to Kierkegaard's ethical stage than to the religious." But his attempt to legitimate this emphasis in his own proposal by suggesting that, "even in Kierkegaard," the ethical stage retains "a certain conceptual predominance" over the religious is untenable, as it ignores (1) Kierkegaard's statement that he was from the beginning an essentially religious author, (2) the distinction between the ethical and Christian discipleship as imitation, and (3) that the ethical is merely a transitional stage to the religious. The primary oversight, however, concerns that feature of Kierkegaard's dialectic by which these very distinctions are thrown into the starkest contrast, namely, the sin-faith antithesis, which, it must be said, upholds with remarkable coherence the biblical account of the fall and the association between sin and knowledge, specifically, the apparently "ethical" knowledge of good and evil.

47. *TM*, 428; see also Dunning, "Paradoxes in Interpretation," 137.

personal qualifications of or resemblance to the original, to the "proto-type." Thus, Christ the mediator, or the Redeemer-Prototype, is reduced to language as "the middle ground in which understanding and agree-ment . . . take place between two people."[48] In contrast to Christian faith, where to be "in Christ" is to be "in faith," or even to "dwell in the house of the LORD," Gadamer's hermeneutic views language as "the house of being" (to employ the language of the later Heidegger). In contrast to the revelatory locus of the self before God as we find it in Kierkegaard,[49] language is the primary place for the disclosure of truth, specifically in the linguistic encounter between the self and the *world*.[50] "The herme-neutical experience is then not just one among many other human ex-periences, but (it) represents *the singular opportunity* for human beings to approach truth."[51] Mediation is no longer cruciform, but language performs its mediating task in the form of *conversation*. Thus, while the only discernible evidence of a qualitative dialectic in Gadamer's thought derives from his appeal to the Incarnation of the Logos, his universal linguistic claims are again and again made on behalf of an "*ana*-logos."

Regarding pneumatology, however, we find no similar appeal to the role of the Holy Spirit, the Spirit of Truth. Rather, Gadamer's pro-posal stakes absolutely everything on the designation "hermeneutical." In light of the grand claims made here for the universal and universally constitutive power of language whereby the word "brings the thing to presentation,"[52] one would expect that the correlation to Christ would require a more consistent and corresponding (divinely speaking) pneumatic analogy. What we have instead, with the use of the all-en-compassing, meta-critical term *hermeneutical*, is an implicit appeal to the Hermes myth, with the apparent contrary assumption that nothing negative may be presented or rendered thereby. Thus, we should not be surprised by Richard Bernstein's contention that "although the concept of truth"—as opposed to method—"is basic to Gadamer's entire proj-ect of philosophical hermeneutics, it turns out to be one of the most

---

48. *TM*, 245–46.

49. See Kierkegaard's definition of the self as spirit in *Sickness unto Death*, 13–15.

50. Thiselton cites Gadamer's *Philosophical Hermeneutics*, 434, when he states: "Language is 'where "I" and world meet.'" Thiselton, *New Horizons*, 323.

51. Jeanrond, *Theological Hermeneutics*, 66–67.

52. *TM*, 410; see also Dunning, "Paradoxes in Interpretation," 136.

elusive concepts in his work . . . It is much easier to say what 'truth' does not mean than to give a positive account."[53] In other words, where we would expect such a broad and sweeping meta-critical proposal to actually propose some criteria for discernment, especially in light of its use of a Christological figure for its understanding of language, in fact, Gadamer's proposal forgets to "knot the thread" by failing to draw upon a corresponding biblical view of critical normativity and spiritual discernment in relation to the Spirit of Truth (Matt 16:16–17; 1 Cor 12:3; Heb 4:12–13; 1 John 4:1; et al.), and instead hitches its slippery analogies to a will-o'-the-wisp.

Hermes, we recall, is "the god of commerce, invention, cunning, and theft, who also served as messenger and herald for the other gods."[54] In his Roman guise as Mercury, he is the god who "served as messenger to the other gods and was himself the god of commerce, travel, and thievery."[55] His name is also given to "any of several weedy plants of the genera *Mercurialis* or *Acalypha*."[56] The adjectival form, *mercurial* not only refers to this god and the planet so named for him, but it describes one "having the characteristics of eloquence, shrewdness, swiftness, and thievishness attributed to [the god Mercury]," "being quick and change-able in character,"[57] "active; lively; sprightly; volatile;" "fickle; flighty; erratic."[58] With reference to the silvery element *mercury*, we find the nounal form, *mercurialism*, which is defined as "poisoning caused by mercury or its components."[59]

Although the name of Hermes seems to be at the root of the verb *diermeneuein* in Luke 24:27 (see also Acts 9:36; 1 Cor 12:30; 14:5, 13, 27, and a nounal form in 1 Cor 14:28), the possibility of the verb's in-forming interpretive normativity, one would think, should focus on the fact that (1) the risen Christ himself is speaking, (2) is speaking about

---

53. Cited in Thiselton, *New Horizons*, 315. Thiselton goes on to summarize Bernstein's point: "On the one hand, Gadamer makes much of developing a particular understanding of Aristotle's practical wisdom (*phronesis*); . . . but on the other hand, he leaves us with the question: What is the basis for our critical judgments?"

54. *AHD*, 607; italics mine.

55. Ibid, 787.

56. Ibid.

57. Ibid, 786.

58. *Random House College Dictionary*, 836.

59. *AHD*, 786.

himself, and (3) is identifying intimations of his coming and his presence specifically in the Hebrew scriptures. (Interestingly, in his journals, Kierkegaard asserts that the resurrection speeches of Christ represent his first *direct* communication, his apparent incognito and the disciple's failure to recognize him notwithstanding.)

In the New Testament, the "person" of Hermes is mentioned only once. Significantly, this occurs in Acts (14:8–18), where the people of Lystra begin to worship Barnabas and Paul as Zeus and Hermes. Paul they mistake for Hermes since he does all the talking (v. 12), to which both apostles passionately and emphatically object by tearing their clothes and crying, "Friends, why are you doing this? We are mortals just like you, and *we bring you good news, that you should turn from these worthless things to the living God*, who made the heaven and the earth and the sea and all that is in them" (vv. 14–18). My concern is less quasi-metaphysical, less with the "person" or "spirit" or "god" known as Hermes/Mercury, than with the interpretive freight implied by the Hermes analogy, which, in the case of a homiletical pneumatology of preaching, simply does not apply.[60] For instance, if we view its deceptive characteristics in light of one principle text (Mark 3:20–30) for developing a proper view of Truth by way of "spiritual discernment," the one encountered at the conclusion of *Sickness Unto Death*,[61] then it is apparent that the regnant "hermeneutics of suspicion" to which Gadamer's thought (along with that of others) has given rise itself warrants suspicion.[62] In other words, precisely to the extent that meta-critical hermeneutics obscures or confuses the critical role of the Holy Spirit in the

60. On a similar note, see my "Penitential Homiletic," 138–39 n. 52, where I argue for the "uniquely unique" qualification of Christ as the "character of God" (Heb 1:1–4).

61. Kierkegaard, *Sickness unto Death*, 125, 131.

62. It is worth noting the fact that the influence of Schleiermacher, for instance, on Kierkegaard appears primarily (1) outside Kierkegaard's authorship proper, in *Concept of Irony*, by way of Schleiermacher's six-volume translation of Plato; and (2) within Kierkegaard's lower pseudonymous authorship, in *Concept of Anxiety*, in the deliberative prologue to a dogmatic treatment of hereditary sin. For this, the pseudonymous author, Vigilius Haufniensis, relies on Schleiermacher's *Glaubenslehre*. While in the text proper, mention is made of Schleiermacher only once, and then in appreciation of his fundamental 'hermeneutical' characteristic that he "spoke only of what he knew," nevertheless, this is in reference to his "immortal service" to *dogmatics*. See Kierkegaard, *Concept of Anxiety*, 20, 228–30, 244. I have found no evidence to suggest that Kierkegaard was familiar with Schleiermacher's lectures on hermeneutics. In addition to Schleiermacher's *Glaubenslehre*, *Über die Religion*, and several volumes of sermons, Kierkegaard owned the volume of *Sämmtliche Werke* containing the *Dialektik*, edited by L. Jonas (Berlin, 1839).

task of spiritual discernment and the proper criteria for proclaiming Christ as the Truth, the occasion calls for swift and decisive renunciation and correction. In Kierkegaardian terms, it is no less than to charge the Spirit of Truth with untruth, by creating a false association between faith and sin, between the Truth himself and the Father of Lies (John 8:44). To pursue the analogy to its logical conclusion, one is faced with the starkest and most dreadful Either/Or.

It is no exaggeration to say that the present state of what is now called hermeneutics was forecast by Kierkegaard long ago as he diagnosed the case of Adler under the subtitle "the religious confusion of the present age." His own prescription for the gnostic Hegelian was to simmer down, sit quietly, and educate himself more thoroughly in Christian concepts.[63] It was a penitential act or "task" to which Kierkegaard applied himself in his own self-educating authorship. More broadly, it formed the basis for the call to reform he issued in his own generation, the call that has become known as the "attack on Christendom;" nevertheless, it was an attack conducted with the knowledge that his voice would have to await the reception of later generations, as witness the early Barth's reception and his repetition of the reformatory "Ad fontes!"

To conclude, a proper understanding of contemporaneity must proceed not only from the qualitative distinction between eternity and temporal endurance, but also by way of a clearer understanding of the question of agency[64] as this is articulated within the proper sphere: Who, or what spirit, is presumed to be and is actually contemporaneous with the person in faith? Further, we should ask, has it been made sufficiently clear that contemporaneity occurs precisely *in* the sphere of faith, that, as Kierkegaard said, contemporaneity *is* faith, faith in the risen Crucified One who alone may be said to be present as Truth in the eternal-temporal dialectic, in the situation of contemporaneity?

To state the matter as plainly as possible, it is one thing for Gadamer to undercut all hermeneutical hopes for a method that will guarantee

---

63. Kierkegaard, *Book on Adler*, 111.

64. I am not concerned so much with sorting out questions of agency within the Godhead, since, as Barth says, the Word and Spirit cannot be separated, but, when it comes to borrowing from non-theological disciplines, with the introduction of potentially distorting and deceptive "spirits" (as these are discerned in matters of both ethics and doctrine) that we admit to the processes of interpretation for proclamation, dogmatic testing, and the development of homiletical strategies.

results and to raise the issue of the unpredicability of conversation that may be likened to play. Where preaching stands in need of a proper understanding of the role of prayer and the agency of the Holy Spirit, however, matters that hermeneutics (whether methodological or anti-methodological, whether general or specific) consistently sets aside, everything depends on one's addressing the proper "conversation" partner, on rightly identifying, invoking, and naming the divine agent. In many ways, it is a matter of whether the ambiguity inherent in the interpretive process will be controlled or uncontrolled. What is needed, I would argue from a Reformed theological perspective, is a fifth *sola*, one that applies to scriptural interpretation: *Sola Sanctus Spiritus*. Viewed in these terms, Kierkegaard's view of contemporaneity is "infinitely" better equipped to assist Christian proclamation than is Gadamer's understanding of the concept. For only when contemporaneity is understood in light of the role of the Holy Spirit and faith—faith as gift, as sphere, as Truth—can the preacher say with the apostle, on the one hand, that "we are not peddlers of God's word like so many; but in Christ we speak as persons of sincerity, as persons sent from God and standing in his presence" (2 Cor 2:17), and on the other, "just as we have the same spirit of faith that is in accordance with scripture—'I believed, and so I spoke'—we also believe, and so we speak, because we know that the one who raised the Lord Jesus will raise us also with Jesus, and will bring us with you into his presence" (2 Cor 4:13–14).

3

"Enter Through the Narrow Gate!"

On the Content of Christian Preaching

Introduction

Everything speaks. Everything, even silence, says something. But silence is not nothing. Silence is something. Nothing does not speak. "There are doubtless many different kinds of sounds in the world, and nothing is without sound" (1 Cor 14:10). To the Pharisees who, on that first Palm Sunday demanded that Jesus rebuke his disciples, our Lord replied, "I tell you, if these become silent, the stones will cry out!" (Luke 19:39–40).

But if everything speaks, what then is preaching? What does Christian preaching say that other speech does *not* say, or more precisely, what words can the preacher speak which conform to the Word of the very God who has summoned the preacher to speak? If Jesus himself taught only what he was sent to teach (John 7:16; see also 4:34; 5:19; 6:37–38; 8:26; Luke 4:43); if the Holy Spirit has been sent to us not to "speak on his own," but to remind us of what Jesus has already said and to "speak whatever he hears" (John 14:26; 16:13); if Paul would curse an angel from heaven or anyone else, including himself, who would preach a gospel contrary to the one which he first proclaimed (Gal 1:18); if the summary of the Torah would threaten with the fate of Baal (Deut 4:1–6) and the final warning of Revelation would add plagues to, or take away the share in the tree of life and the holy city (Rev 22:18–19) from, anyone who would alter the commandments or the prophecies of the LORD, what then *is* the preacher able to say which does not add to or take away from the content of Christian preaching? Our opening questions are thus in a certain sense *epistemological*, that is, they are concerned with "how we know what we know," "how we know the Truth." What is the nature of the wisdom, the intelligence, the understanding (*epistemon*; Jas 3:13; cf. 1 Cor 1:20–27), to which and with which we are to speak?

Our epistemological questions require us to discern between the worldly and the godly, between the present age and the age to come, between the inferior wisdom of the world and the superior foolishness of God that we know through the saving faith of Christ. In the final analysis, however, they require us to distinguish between the *epistemic* and the *pistic*, between epistemology itself and faith.

This discourse on the content of Christian preaching will take up in turn three *epistemic* standpoints, *each* of which will require us to identify three essential *tensions*, or more properly, *dialectics*, that, ubiquitous in scripture, impinge directly on the possibility of our clear discernment at these standpoints. In other words, each standpoint requires the piercing scrutiny of our "eyes to see" and the acute attention of our "ears to hear." Briefly, these *three standpoints* from which we must consider our calling to preach are, if I may so organize them: (1) the place *from* which we are called out, that is, *the present age*, (2) the sphere *into* which we are called, namely, *the age to come*, and (3) that way of suffering, the "groaning gate" *through* which all are called, the way of the Spirit that Christianity proclaims as the *only* way between these two ages, namely, the narrow way of the cross on which was crucified the true content of Christian preaching.

The general thrust of this argument is admittedly rhetorical, concerned with moving people, yet it makes use of dialectical categories to exert its pressure externally, that is, it is mindful of externals such as culture, context, and the cross. Rhetoric and dialectic, as Luther has reminded us, are inseparable (see *LW* 27:24). But time will not permit us here to consider the converse application of rhetorical categories to the general field of dialectics, that is, we will not here concern ourselves with the movement of meaning within the text, which, Christianly understood, pertains to the movement of the Holy Spirit through the Word of God. This question is that of biblical interpretation, which today is often and almost universally confused with hermeneutics. Hermeneutics also concerns itself with external context and internal dynamics such as linguistics, but also has the habit of reaching into every other sphere of inquiry as well. Because we are concerned as preachers with proclaiming the Word of God as we are inspired, guided, instructed, reminded, and empowered by the Holy Spirit, we do well to remember that homiletics, preaching, and ministers of the Word and Sacrament are, first of all, to "test the spirits," to distinguish between, on the one hand, potentially deceptive influences that bear the trademark of Hermes, and on the other hand, the Spirit of the Lord "whose name is Jealous"

(Exod 34:14; cf. 20:5; Deut 4:24; 5:9–10; 6:14–15; 32: 16, 19, 21; Josh 24:19; Job 36:33; Ps 79:5; Ezek 36:6; 39:25; Nah 1:2; Zech 1:14; 8:1–2). Clearly there are many spirits at work in the world, many "gods" judging unjustly and favoring the wicked, sending garbled and confused messages by this fleet-footed mercurial spirit, the messenger of the gods, for whom hermeneutics is named. But . . .

> God has taken his place in the divine council;
> in the midst of the gods he holds judgment:
> "How long will you judge unjustly
> and show partiality to the wicked? [Selah]
> Give justice to the weak and the orphan;
> maintain the right of the lowly and the destitute.
> Rescue the weak and the needy;
> deliver them from the hand of the wicked."
>
> They have neither knowledge nor understanding,
> they walk around in darkness;
> all the foundations of the earth are shaken.
>
> I say, "You are gods,
> children of the Most High, all of you;
> nevertheless, you shall die like mortals,
> and fall like any prince."
>
> Rise up, O God, judge the earth;
> for all the nations belong to you!
> (Psalm 82:1–8)

Surely, there are many voices in both culture and scripture which hermeneutics insists we must hear and consider. Christian theology, however, is not beholden to hermeneutics for this insight. Our adherence to the great commandment (Matt 22:36–38) and our obedient insistence that "the LORD your God is One" (Deut 6:4) must neither be taken to deny or obscure the Christian doctrine of the Trinity, nor turn us into blind guides (Matt 15:14; 23:16, 24) who, in the name of an unqualified monotheism, become senseless and ignorant of and therefore, in the Jungian sense, vulnerable to, "the principalities and powers of this present darkness" (Eph 6:12) and the *stoicheia* of the cosmos, the elemental spirits of the universe (Gal 4:3, 9; Col 2:8, 20). It does not do to nominally profess faith in the Holy Spirit and ignore the impious spirits that contend against our Advocate and Paraclete. To realistically acknowledge the existence of such spirits does not in any way necessitate that one worship them and thus become polytheists. Quite the contrary. The Spirit fully expects we will encounter many perspectives and perceive many voices speaking through the Holy Scripture and within the world and, further, that we will discern them with power, love, and self-discipline (2 Tim 1:7), that we will meet them head on with truth, faith, hope, righteousness, salvation, supplication, alertness, perseverance, and the preaching of the gospel (Eph 6:11–18). For the Spirit also recognizes and testifies one sovereign Word speaking beneath, among, over, above, and through them all. Scripture teaches that there is but one thing needful (Luke 10; Ps 27:4), only one teacher (Matt 23:8), and it summons us to sit at the feet of *this* one, to seek the face of *this* one, to harken to the familiar voice of *this* Good Shepherd who calls each by name (John 10:3).

About this much more will need to be said, but for now let us "consider (our) own call" (1 Cor 1:26), namely, that we are called out of this present age, this present darkness (Eph 6:12), from our frequently weak, usually foolish, often less than noble, but certainly diverse points of departure.

§1. The Present Age: Esthetic Diversity in Creation and Culture

"Consider your own call, brothers and sisters." *First*, consider that *from* which you have been called. Consider the fact that we have each set out from our own various points of departure, from diverse situations in this present age, from our own particular life circumstances in which we each found ourselves being addressed by the one Word of God. Are we not situated in the midst of tremendous diversity in both God's creation and human culture? Human life in temporality must ever receive our careful attention, our pastoral compassion, our humble respect. Bewildering diversity, sometimes delightful, sometimes daunting, meets us at every turn. Broadly speaking, however, diversity meets us in two distinct guises that form the complementary poles about which we shall begin to discern our first three dialectics. These *poles of diversity* pertain to *creation* and *culture*.

The *diversity of creation* is a prominent theme in scripture. In the Old Testament we find it in the creation narrative (Gen 1–3); in the account of Adam's naming the species (Gen 3), in Noah's preserving them (Gen 6–9), in the wide-eyed reports of the spies who were sent to assess the land of promise (Num 14), in the voice that spoke to Job from the whirlwind (Job 38–42), in numerous psalms (65, 104, et al.) and the wisdom literature. In the New Testament we read of the diversity of creation in several passages, though perhaps most important among them is 1 Cor 15 (where the apostle's purpose is to *contrast* the glory of this created diversity, as we shall attempt to do, with that which is "of first importance" (v. 3), namely, the destiny of Christ Jesus and the supreme glory of his resurrection. "Not all flesh is alike, but there is one flesh for human beings, another for animals, another for birds, and another for fish. There are both heavenly bodies and earthly bodies, but the glory of the heavenly is one thing, and that of the earthly is another. There is one glory of the sun, and another glory of the moon, and another glory of the stars; indeed, star differs from star in glory" (1 Cor 15:39–41). Yes, *everything speaks.* "The heavens are telling the glory of God; and the firmament proclaims his handiwork" (Ps 19:1).

Diverse cultures are also well-represented in scripture. Furthermore, the Lord himself has had a hand in creating them (Ps 86:8–9). Their cultures are not absolutely of their own design and not utterly without God (Rom 1:19–20). Nevertheless, the Old Testament is clearly concerned throughout with Hebrew, Israelite, and Judaic "culture," from the most literal sense in which it prescribes the forms of Israel's ancient rites and ceremonies pertaining to their worship in tabernacle and temple, to the most mundane descriptions of daily life. The reason for this is unambiguous from a New Testament perspective, "for salvation is from the Jews" (John 4:22). Many other nations and cultures, along with their practices and their prejudices, are also mentioned in the pages of scripture, though admittedly, these are often (but not always) depicted in a negative light and proscribed according to the prohibition of idolatry. From its faint glimmer in the Old Testament (Isa 42:6), God's mission through Israel to the Gentile nations breaks into a major theme in the New Testament (Matt 28:16–20; Acts 1:8; 13:47; et al.) and becomes a cultural and theological flashpoint, as covenantal signs such as circumcision, linguistic issues involving proclamation in new tongues, and dietary laws regarding, say, sacrificed meat and picking grain on the Sabbath, all become critical moments of discernment and decision for the church. Clearly the Bible does not naively assume a worldview of cultural homogeneity.

Nevertheless, we must posit this rule: *culture and context are everywhere operative, but nowhere determinative; everywhere legitimate, but nowhere ultimate.* Scripture distinguishes between these two poles of diversity, that is, between diversity in creation and diversity in culture, in this way. In creation, God exercises ultimate freedom, which includes, of course, inspiring humans to acts of imitative, poetic creativity. But in creation, *God* is sovereign over creation's diverse forms, genuses, and species, whereas, in culture, God freely allows *humans* to exercise dominion (Gen 1:26–28; 2:19). This does not prohibit the Spirit of God from working in and through and upon human culture, but it is in culture, not in creation as such, that humans have their primary freedom and influence.

We must note briefly, however, the many ways in which God's creation and human culture shape one another directly. On the one hand, human influence on the environment ranges from primitive earthworks to modern architectural wonders, and with the exercise of this influence, humans bear responsibility for their impact on agriculture, the land, the waterways, and the atmosphere. On the other hand, the creation shapes human cultures to a considerable extent with its concentrations of specific natural resources, with its varying degrees of fertility and precipitation favoring certain crops, its inhabitability favoring certain livestock, in particular places and not in others. A tremendous amount of what we know as human culture revolves around what crops people are able to cultivate in their respective backyards, what they are able to fish from their waters, what animals they are able to feed and breed and butcher and cure in an affordable and sanitary manner.

Since Genesis 3, we humans have worked the fields to feed ourselves by the sweat of our brows. Human cultures cultivate those foods and produce those fabrics that distinguish the continent, the sector of creation, the turf on which they dwell. Yes, God creates and reigns over creation. Humans create and exercise dominion through culture, but consider how much of human culture is defined by the esthetic [*esthien* = to eat], how overwhelmingly culture is concerned with "the cares of the pagans," how much of our ethnicity (whether we are clustered in a relative majority or a relative minority) is consumed with consuming: "What shall we eat or what shall we drink?" Consider how much culture is wrapped up in its clothing, "What shall we wear?" (Matt 6:31) Are these not the questions which culture has, in large part, asked and answered for us? Does not every travel guide, regardless of the destination under consideration, provide us with ample descriptions of cultural forms, and in a certain sense, define the culture, precisely by means of such esthetic terms?

It is for this reason that we must respectfully, but honestly and critically, identify this first standpoint with Kierkegaard's *esthetic* sphere or what Luther termed "the natural way" (*LW* 26:267). To the *esthetic* stage of *the present age* we will apply three dialectical tensions that must ever be observed and must never be allowed to fall into disuse, as they have done in recent decades. These enduring dialectics are those:

(1) between *the Creator and the creature*, (2) between *eternity and temporality*; and (3) between *the Johannine "world" of sin and the Pauline definition of faith* (Rom 14:23).

§1.1 *The Divine/Human Dialectic: God's Ways Are Not Our Ways*

Everything speaks, but not everything speaks the Word of God. God's thoughts and words and ways are not the human creature's thoughts and words and ways (Isa 55:8-9). This most basic theological distinction, yet the one which egocentric human beings are most quick to deny, ignore, and forget, is the radical distinction between the Creator and the creature.

> Claiming to be wise, they became fools; and they exchanged the glory of the immortal God for images resembling a mortal human being or birds or four-footed animals or reptiles. Therefore God gave them up in the lusts of their hearts to impurity, to the degrading of their bodies among themselves, because they exchanged the truth about God for a lie and worshiped and served the creature rather than the Creator, who is blessed forever! Amen. (Rom 1:22-25)

Idolatry is everywhere and consistently denounced in scripture (Exod 20:4-6; 34:17; Lev 19:4; 26:1; 2 Kgs 17:9-15; Pss 31:6; 106:36-38; 115:4-8; 2 Cor 6:16; 1 John 5:21; et al). Surely the reasons for this consistent providential prohibition are manifold and can neither be fully grasped by human wisdom nor treated fully here. We should at least, however, observe and bear in mind the relative ease with which human beings are seduced by it, in part, because idolatry can and does take countless diverse forms.

Indeed, idolatry is so prevalent that the righteous proto-Christological figure of Elihu, the one primary character in the Book of Job who does *not* earn God's rebuke, can say with certainty in his own response to Job: "Surely God is great, and we do not know him" (Job 36:26a). It is highly ironic, in light of our fallen human tendency to idolize familiar forms, that Jesus can say to the Samaritan woman at the well: "You worship what you do not know; we worship what we know, for salvation is from the Jews" (John 4:22). In other words, in the act of idolatry, humans worship something or someone familiar to them in such a way that they clearly do not know what they are doing or what spirit or spirits they are entertaining or worshiping. But when we give due praise and worship and adoration to the invisible, and in the autonomous, rationalistic, humanistic sense, the *unknowable* God, we are assured by the Lord Jesus that we worship what we know! No wonder idolatry persists in the face of such confusion! How can the Creator be given due glory when the creature continually confuses him or herself or the fellow creature with the Creator? This ancient pantheistic heresy must be clearly condemned in every age as it was by Pope Clement V, who in his papal bull, *Ad nostrum* (1311), denounced it under the telling designation of the Heresy of the Free Spirit [see Friesen, *Thomas Muentzer,* 90 94; Leff, *Heresy in the Middle Ages,* 2 vols.].

On the other hand, we are much better able to guard against this heresy if we rigourously maintain what Kierkegaard in the nineteenth century described as the "infinite qualitative difference" between God and humanity. This distinction found expression in the twentieth century in Karl Barth's description of God as "wholly other," that is, *other than the creature!* Clearly, our knowledge of God absolutely depends on God's self-revelation, which cannot be received by the creature who fails to respect both the radical *objective* difference which must ever persist between the creature and the Creator and the absolute necessity of the creature's *subjection* or *subjectivity in relation* to the sovereignty of God. Consider two gospel texts, one in which Jesus labels as Satanic the fixation of the mind on human things rather than divine things (Mark 8:33), and the other in which he denies any further explanatory revelations regarding his authority to those who cannot or will not decide whether John's baptism was from above or of human origin (Mark 11:29–33). In both cases, the *divine/human dialectic* is at issue. In both cases, divine revelation is juxtaposed with a human fixation, and even a Satanic obsession, with the creaturely and the cultural sphere.

Consider as well a passage in John's gospel where "Judas (not Iscariot)" asked Jesus directly about the manner of his self-revelation: "Lord, *how is it that you will reveal yourself to us,* and not to the world?" (John 14:22). At first glance, Jesus seems to ignore the question altogether, since his reply is nearly identical with his words that prompted Jude's question in the first place. They are a virtual *verbatim* repetition. Why would John bother to record Jude's question at all if Jesus was only going to ignore it? On further consideration, however, what we discover is that, in both cases, Jesus answers the question regarding his self-revelation very directly:

> *"They who have my commandments and keep them are those who love me*; and those who love me will be loved by my Father, and

I will love them and reveal myself to them." Judas (not Iscariot) said to him, "Lord, how is it that you will reveal yourself to us, and not to the world?" Jesus answered him, "Those who love me will *keep my word*, and my Father will love them, and we will come to them and make our home with them. *Whoever does not love me does not keep my words; and the word that you hear is not mine, but is from the Father who sent me.* (John 14:21–24; emphasis mine)

Jesus goes on in such a way as to show clearly that what is to be expected and discerned in the moment of revelation is not doctrinal innovation, but faithfulness to the unchanged and unchanging word of God:

> "I have said these things to you while I am still with you. But the Advocate, the Holy Spirit, whom the Father will send in my name, will teach you everything, and *remind you of all that I have said to you.*" (John 14:25–26; emphasis mine)

Clearly, the very possibility of our receiving revelation *of* the Lord *from* the Lord, *of* the Truth *from* the Spirit of Truth, is put at risk when we fail to respect at all times the "infinite qualitative difference" between the "wholly other" God and the cultured human creature. The words of the Lord are to be heard and kept, for they come to us not by simply arising within us, as though we were their source and author, or as though the human biblical writers simply penned them out of their own esthetic genius, but they come to us from without. Indeed, they must come *extra nos*, for God's thoughts and words and ways are *not* human thoughts and words and ways (Isa 55:8–9). "Therefore we must pay greater attention to what we have heard, so that we do not drift away from it" (Heb 2:1).

§1.2 The Eternal/Temporal Dialectic: We Press On Toward the Goal

Everything speaks. And what is more, our words endure far beyond what our ears alone perceive, far beyond what even our longest memories can recollect to consciousness after a great span of time. Our words are heard by God and by those around us. Scripture warns that we will have to render an accounting for every careless word (Matt 12:36). Our words endure far beyond our estimation. Therefore, they deserve to be considered thoroughly, chosen carefully, and only then spoken reverently, lovingly, and in the fear of the Lord. Yet our words are not eternal words: ". . . as for prophecies, they will come to an end; as for tongues, they will cease; as for knowledge, it will come to an end" (1 Cor 13:8b). Our words, like heaven and earth, will pass away (Matt 24:35; Mark 13:31; Luke 21:33), but, like love, which never ends (1 Cor 13:8a), the words of the Lord, "will not pass away." No, "the word of the Lord endures forever. That word is the good news that was announced to you" (1 Pet 1:25).

The *second* dialectical tension that exerts pressure on the esthetic sphere is thus the tension between the eternal and the temporal, between that which endures unchanging, the immortal, and that which is mortal and undergoes the radical change of death. Clearly, while these two categories pertain respectively to the divine and the human, we cannot identify them simplistically so as to obscure questions posed by the doctrines of resurrection, eschatology and final judgment. Despite our keen sense of the passage of time and our marking of time in the cycles of the daily rhythms of the rising and the setting of the sun, in the cycles of the weekly sabbath, the lunar month, the sequence of the seasons, the feast and fast days of the liturgical year, the measuring of eras in terms of decades, centuries, epochs, millenia, and even significant astronomical events, Christianity does *not* finally hold to a cyclic view of history, but understands these rotations as part of a greater movement, like the revolutions of Ezekiel's wheel that moves swiftly, directly, purposefully bound for a particular destination, a *telos*, a goal. Paganism views time as an endless sequence of such cycles. There is no *telos*, no destination, for the many and varied forms of paganism, there is only rotation, as though the wheel of time were simply spinning, but never advancing. Such is not the view of Christianity, which understands the temporal cycles as part of the world's movement toward God's fulfillment of the divine plan for salvation and the redemption of all things, a *telos* that takes eternity as its ultimate reference, but ever insists, in temporality, on the distinction between time and eternity.

If the verse we cited earlier from Elihu's rebuke of Job identifies the infinite qualitative difference between the divine and the human, we should also note, in parallel fashion, that it names the present distinction: "Surely God is great, and we do not know him; *the number of his years is unsearchable*" (Job 36:26). But the human, at best, stands with the psalmist who prays thus: "So teach us to count our days that we may gain a wise heart" (Ps 90:12).

Consider the divine summons to proclamation issued to the prophet of hope. The fortieth chapter of the major prophet and the first of that literary section known as Second Isaiah (Isa 40–55) is the source of the distant echo with which all four New Testament gospels begin, the voice crying out in the wilderness to make a straight way for the LORD (Isa 40:3–5). But as both James (1:11–12) and 1 Peter (1:24–25) remind us, the content of the proclamation the prophet is called to preach is not immediately clear to him.

> A voice says, "Cry out!"
>   And I said, "What shall I cry?"
> All people are grass,
>   their constancy is like the flower of the field.
> The grass withers, the flower fades,
>   when the breath of the LORD blows upon it;
>   surely the people are grass.
> The grass withers, the flower fades;
>   but the word of our God will stand forever.
> (Isa 40:6–8)

Thus, the preacher who is faithful to the content of Christian preaching will not only *not* deny the reality of death and the fact of human temporality, but will be constantly aware of these harsh realities, even as the preacher qualifies, critiques, and denies their finality in light of eternity. What hope of heaven can we expect our listeners to have if we ignore the constant threat to life of which time itself reminds us, the threat that time itself poses to us? What hope of eternal life, if the fading and withering of our mortal bodies is ever masked by what atheist Ernest Becker called the denial of death, to say nothing of cosmetic surgery and the cult of the body?

No, in order for us to arrive at the content of Christian preaching, we must ask with the prophet, "What shall I cry?" and hear with fearless, faithful, dialectical discernment, that there is here again an "infinite qualitative difference" between the immortal God and us mortal creatures, between the eternal word and our enduring, but temporal words. Yet we do so in light of another amazing paradox, namely, that preaching lends a temporal, human voice to the eternal, divine Word, the very Word that, according to the concluding chapter of that same prophet of hope, will not return to God empty, but "shall accomplish that which (the LORD) purpose(s), and succeed in the thing for which (God) sent it!" (Isa 55:10–11).

§1.3 The Faith/Sin Dialectic: A Theological Solution for the Anthropological Problem

Hermeneutics has reminded us that we shape reality profoundly by our use of words in temporality. Yet, does Christianity depend on hermeneutics for this insight? Not at all. As Kierkegaard has rightly noted, Christianity always says, and will never cease to say, "Let it be with you *as* you believe" (Matt 8:13).[1] As God speaks creation into being, we too find that our speech shapes the reality we inhabit. Our words are not God's words. Yet they do have their long-lasting, if temporary, effect. Indeed, our words speak to the very nature and the state of our faith or our unfaith. More precisely, they reveal either our faith or our sin!

Why do we contrast faith and sin? Is not sin the opposite of righteousness, faith the opposite of doubt? Here we must return to our understanding of the *esthetic* sphere in which we are operating and to the dialectical pressures that we must discern and apply to move beyond it. In fact, the dialectic of faith and sin applies not *within* the esthetic sphere, but is the very dialectic between the esthetic life and true faith, between our former and our eschatological existence.

Perhaps a brief review of Kierkegaard's *spheres of existence* is needed here,[2] which we will illumine by an example, namely, our understanding of sin. In the *esthetic* sphere, *sin* may be defined as *ugliness*, or quite literally, *bad form*. In the *ethical* stage, which Kierkegaard understood as a transitional sphere between the esthetic and the religious, sin takes on the meaning with which we are most familiar. Sin, in light of ethics and morality, is juridical sin, a conviction of guilt, illegal behavior, immoral conduct. *Christian faith, however, is a leap beyond the ethical.* Faith originates with Abraham's obedience, his willingness to "teleologically suspend" the ethical and do the unthinkable, to raise the knife over Isaac, the son of his and Sarah's old age, his "only" son whom he loves,

---

1. Kierkegaard himself laid emphasis on the word "as," so as to stress the sense of simultaneity. "See, this is the struggle of faith in which you can have an occasion to be tried and tested every day. The Gospel is not the Law; the Gospel will not save you by rigorousness but by leniency; but this leniency will save you, it will not deceive you; therefore there is rigorousness in it." Kierkegaard, *Works of Love*, 378–80; see also 464.

2. Kierkegaard himself explained that the stages were employed throughout his authorship. See, e.g., "A Glance at Contemporary Effort in Danish Literature," in *Concluding Unscientific Postscript* [J. Climacus, pseud.], 251–300, and the concise classification of the Sophists in *Stages on Life's Way* [F. Taciturnus, pseud.], 486–87.

who is to inherit the promises of God.[3] What then can sin mean in relation to such faith? No relation at all. Mutual exclusion. In *Sickness Unto Death*, Kierkegaard takes Paul to be offering a clear definition of faith: "whatever does not proceed from faith is sin" (Rom 14:23b).[4]

Such a reading is amply confirmed in scripture in such a way that we can safely say that faith has nothing to do with our deeds as such, but that all of our deeds, are tainted with sin: "We have all become like one who is unclean, / and all our righteous deeds are like a filthy cloth. / We all fade like a leaf, / and our iniquities, like the wind, take us away" (Isa 64:6). "But the scripture has imprisoned all things under the power of sin, so that what was promised through faith in Jesus Christ might be given to those who believe" (Gal 3:22). "For God has imprisoned all in disobedience so that he may be merciful to all" (Rom 11:32). While we must ever guard against turning faith itself into a work by which we save ourselves, we must also recognize that, when asked what works we are to do, Jesus answered in terms of faith. "This is the work of God, that you believe in him whom he has sent" (John 6:29).

Thus, in the most severe and all-inclusive sense of the term, sin is everything that precedes the leap of faith, everything that falls short of it, everything that prevents it, everything that balks at it. Sin and faith are opposites, so that the entire esthetic realm *is* sin, is the *world* as the Johannine literature views it, as is every lapse back into the esthetic. As for *ethics*, all the works done apart from faith, all attempts at humanistic social ethics that come short of the leap . . . all of these are "sin." As alarming as this may sound, is this not the clear implication of Calvin's first use of the law? Is not the law, as Luther said, the hammer which drives us to Christ? "For whoever keeps the whole law but fails in one point has become accountable for all of it!" (Jas 2:10)

Despite all we have said concerning the glory of God, the wonderful diversity of God's creation and the widely varying customs in different lands, distant times, foreign tongues, diverse cultures; despite all of this, hermeneutics is not prepared to address this final dialectic between faith and sin. It knows only the first two definitions of sin: esthetic ugliness and ethical failure. Hermeneutics is concerned with horizontal relationality, with the comparative relativity of human perspectives, with differences in class, culture, race, and gender, with interpretive maneuvers that inhere in the process of linguistic translation. Hermeneutics is most offended when bad form arrives as either the

---

3. Kierkegaard, *Fear and Trembling* [J. Silentio, pseud.].

4. Kierkegaard, *Sickness unto Death* [Anti-Climacus, pseud.], 82.

ugly or the impolite. At its best, hermeneutics aspires to social ethics, but ethics is hermeneutics' highest good, "a positive doctrine of obligation, instead of repentance being the supreme task of the ethical and expressly negative."[5] Ethics, not the rigorousness of repentant faith, is the *telos* of hermeneutics and dialogue is its default method, whether it espouses the term or not (as in the case of Gadamer).

The preached Word of God *also* addresses human beings in their particular situations. Preaching is ever attuned to the specific sociocultural, economic, linguistic, political context into which it heralds the Word. Yet preaching also knows that *every* human situation, despite its singular particularities, is itself contextually enmeshed in the *universal* anthropological predicament of *sin*. Long before hermeneutics has exhausted itself with endless comparisons of one human perspective with another, one truth claim with another, one worldview with another and another and another *ad infinitum*, long before the most committed celebrants of diversity are able to gasp and pant that their competing hermeneutical insights can never be exhausted, preaching knows that something is still dreadfully, horribly wrong with the celebration of senseless comparisons (2 Cor 10:12). Unless the world reaches a point of hermeneutical exhaustion, however, it will not remain silent long enough to hear the preacher clear her throat and offer her theological term for this universal situation. "When the Son of Man comes, will he find faith on earth, faith that is the opposite of sin?" At which the din of hermeneutical protestations and relativistic objections will no doubt begin again.

Preaching knows, however, that taking offense is not the *only* response to the Word of God. Preaching knows that *faith* comes by hearing (Rom 10:1–17), faith that is itself the theological solution to the anthropological problem of *sin* that has troubled both creature and culture since Genesis 3. It is this dialectical tension between *sin and faith* that demands of both the discerning preacher and the responsive listener that they serve only one master (Matt 6:24). The dialectic of faith and sin is that which clearly sets before the listener the ultimatum of Joshua: "Now if you are unwilling to serve the LORD, choose this day whom you will serve" (Josh 24:15). "I call heaven and earth to witness against you today that I have set before you life and death, blessings and

5. Kierkegaard, *Stages on Life's Way*, 486.

curses. Choose life so that you and your descendants may live" (Deut 30:19). Where the blind guide of hermeneutics only blinds us to faith by fixing our attention strictly on esthetics and ethics as human things, preaching insists we cannot rest contented in the hermeneutical confusion of the present age, at least not with impunity, at least not without unthinkable eternal consequences.

Enten-eller, said Kierkegaard's pseudonymous Victor Eremita, the Victorious Hermit. *Either-Or!*, cries the preacher. It is no coincidence that two theologians in our day, Robert Jensen and Carl Braaten, have edited a book of essays which again uses Kierkegaard's title, *Either/Or*, to which they have attached the subtitle, *The Gospel or Neo-Paganism*. We must, of course, not confuse this either-or with the heresy of Pelagianism and semi-Pelagianism, which for decades has run amok in the form of North American "decision theology." The distinction can be easily upheld, if we are rigorously attentive to the dialectic between our decision to attend to the true content of Christian preaching, Jesus Christ and him crucified, who is the sole means of our salvation, and a false soteriology that attributes our salvation to such attention itself. Here again, we might well restate this dialectic in Christo-soteriological terms: Christ's faithful obedience is the means of our salvation *versus* Christ's becoming sin that we might become the righteousness of God (2 Cor 5:21). But here we are anticipating our third (Christological) standpoint, that is, where we find ourselves before the narrow gate. First, we must ask our epistemological questions of what lies beyond that gate, of what we will find in the eschatological age to come, where we live in the eternal, in faith, in Christ.

§2. The Age to Come: *Esthes* in the New Creation and the Kingdom of God

The choice for life, the response of faith, the decisive leap *into* the life of faith, will not permit us to remain at our first standpoint, which hermeneutics as such is incapable of transcending. Faith requires that we both set our minds on the things that are above (Col 3:1–2) and take the gospel to the ends of the earth (Acts 1:8). Faith comes by hearing (Rom 10:17) both the *upward* and the *outward* call, though paradoxically, the response of faith is expressed by a *downward* movement of humility and an *inward* movement of earnest reflection, neither of which, however, must be confused with the *telos* of faith. The Living Word of God, the Good Shepherd, has come forth that we may have abundant new life (John 10:10) in every dimension.

"The LORD is my chosen portion and my cup; you hold my lot. The boundary lines have fallen for me in pleasant places; I have a goodly heritage" (Ps 16:5-6). "Out of my distress I called on the LORD; the LORD answered me and set me in a broad place" (Ps 118:5; see also 18:19; 31:8; 2 Sam 22:20; Job 36:16).

To say the very least, this broad space into which our Shepherd Lord leads us, our ultimate destination, demands our faithful reflection, our spiritual discernment, and most decisively, our actual *departure from* our respective "points of departure"—that is, after all, why we call them that—all of which require the prayer of faith and the gift of the Holy Spirit. "Jesus said, 'No one who puts a hand to the plow and looks back is fit for the kingdom of God'" (Luke 9:62).

Therefore, our *second* point of consideration will be the aim, the purpose, the destination, the *telos*, the goal toward which we as *believers* struggle and press on, toward which as *pastors*, as *under-shepherds* to the Good Shepherd, as *preachers*, as *overseers*, we would usher, urge, encourage, and lead Christ's flock, those regarding whom we are consecrated to the sacred duty of oversight. Here we will consider those diverse characteristics that obtain in the new creation or, in traditional terms, the kingdom of heaven. Here too we will treat three dialectical tensions to which every discerning preacher must carefully attend, namely, the dialectic between (1) *the individual believer and the ecclesial faith community*, (2) on the one hand, *the indwelling by the Holy Spirit* in persons and congregations of faith, and on the other hand, *the sense in which we indwell, take shelter, and are clothed in Christ and his body*; and (3) the spiritual dynamic of signification according to the biblical idiom as this dynamic takes both positive and negative forms, variously deemed in theological literature as *analogy* and *dialectic*, "the rule of *metaphor*" which insists on a certain self-correcting "is not" for every "is" that it posits, *paradox* with its contradictory poles, and finally, *parable* and *disputation*.

It is worth reiterating that, in order to recall the fact that we are dealing here with a radically distinct stage of reflection, that is, in order to prevent our lapsing into the esthetic, we will find ourselves relying heavily on the *regula fidei* and on Kierkegaard's leap of *faith*. In this way we will maintain the distinction between the two kingdoms (to use Luther's terms), the two ages (Kierkegaard), the two cities of the earthly Rome and the New Jerusalem (Augustine's *City of God*). In every case, in each of these dialectics, faith and faithfulness will be of the utmost importance for our epistemological discernment, our rhetorical decisions, our spiritual orientation and biblical interpretation.

In order to address the most immediate and obvious objections hermeneutics will raise, we will gather these various dialectics under one particular sign which will both (1) refute the charge that ethics disappears entirely when faith is upheld as an altogether separate sphere, a charge which is clearly false, and (2) redress a similar objection with regard to esthetics, namely, that such a view of faith is overly critical of beauty and form. Further, our use of this sign will demonstrate the spiritual idiom of scripture which even linguistic hermeneutics cannot penetrate since it is unwilling to be tutored by the one and only qualified Teacher of biblical interpretation. This spiritual symbol with which we refute both claims and assert the reemergence of Christian ethics (in the indicative) and transformed esthetics (in the doxological) is that of "the fine linen [*bussinon*] (which) is the righteous deeds of the saints" (Rev 19:8; see also 18:12, 16; 19:14). This sign, however, is not limited to Christian ethics. Christians are to clothe themselves *not only* with good works, but with Christ himself (Rom 13:13–14) and with the whole spiritual "armour of God" (Eph 6:10–20). The contrast of the present age and the age to come is as stark as that between the Gerasene demoniac under the influence of the legion of demons and the same man, following his deliverance by the Lord, when he was discovered by his neighbors to be *clothed and in his right mind* (Mark 5:1–20): a synonymous parallel construction if there ever was one! In other words, to have the mind of Christ is to be clothed in Christ.

The new clothing (*esthes*) that is characteristic of the *eschaton* is variously described using several terms. It is frequently reported in association with heavenly messengers (Luke 24:4; Acts 1:10; 10:30). It is glimpsed in Christ's transfiguration, seen with even greater clarity in his resurrection, and promised in the New Testament as that with which we are to be adorned in the kingdom. "For in this tent we groan, longing to be clothed with our heavenly dwelling—if indeed, when we have taken it off we will not be found naked. For while we are still in this tent, we groan under our burden, because we wish not to be unclothed but to be further clothed, so that what is mortal may be swallowed up by life" (2 Cor. 5:2-4). In the baptismal ceremonial of the ancient church, fresh robes were wrapped around the newly baptized as they emerged naked from the baptistry, symbolizing their new birth and their being clothed in Christ.

While we cannot in this space exhaust the vast and glorious implications of this metaphor, we can note its absolute necessity with respect to our being prepared for and remaining within the eschatological kingdom (Matt 22:11ff.). Further, we can and must note that, while scripture variously describes the radical newness of life under the sovereignty of God as the *new creation* and the *kingdom of heaven*, we will here consider the *new creation* as that which pertains more clearly to individual regeneration, which seems consistent with Paul's description of it.

> "Therefore, if anyone is in Christ, he is a new creation: everything old has passed away; see, everything has become new!" (2 Cor 5:17). "May I never boast of anything except the cross of our Lord Jesus Christ, by which the world has been crucified to me, and I to the world. For neither circumcision nor uncircumcision is anything; but a new creation is everything!" (Gal 6:14–16)

On the other hand, we will consider the kingdom, the reign of the Sovereign God, as pertaining more to the heavenly realm (since kingdoms are rarely comprised of a single subject), the communion of the saints, which Christ the Son now governs, and which ultimately he will present to God the Father (1 Cor 15:24). In other words, the individual will receive due emphasis in our consideration of the new creation, and the communal in our consideration of the kingdom. Having drawn these general distinctions, let us consider more specifically the three dialectics that must be maintained when preaching the kingdom of heaven.

§2.1 *The Ecclesial/Individual Dialectic: Many Are Called, But Few Are Chosen*

Much has been said in the last half-century regarding the need for theological education to use inclusive language. It is a complex issue that we will not treat in depth here. While the debate concerning inclusive language and the hermeneutics of inclusiveness have yielded many important insights, their rhetorical implications for the practice of preaching have far too often been taken to mean that we must avoid gender-specific language by assuming the priority and adopting the grammar of the collective. As preachers we say *we* and *us* far too often, with the disastrous result that *you* and *you* and *you* and *I* are not addressed, or at least, *we* are given far too much latitude to excuse and exclude ourselves from the intended audience. As Kierkegaard warned, the single individual is the decisive category for the future of Christianity. He did *not*, in fact, advocate indirect communication as a "method" for preaching (as preachers have come to believe), but, when he preached, he spoke directly, intimately, pastorally, to the second person, usually to the singular *you*. No, preaching that only ever addresses the plurality in terms of *we* and *us* presumes a solidarity that, in fact, ignores diversity at the individual level, and worse yet, allows the single individual to either intentionally hide or unintentionally get lost in the crowd.

Neither should the preacher waste valuable time in the attempt to describe every possible circumstance of every single individual in every single sermon. Were the preacher to do so, the gospel would never be proclaimed or heard! *Neither extreme socialistic communitarianism nor a cult of the individual is faithful to the content of Christian preaching.* This is precisely why the relationship between *the individual believer and the church* must ever remain in *dialectical tension*.

Kierkegaard stated it this way: "insofar as there is the *congregation* in the religious sense, this is a concept that lies on the other side of *the single individual*, and that above all must not be confused with what politically can have validity: the public, the crowd, the numerical, etc."[6] Note the strong emphasis on, the high regard for, the single individual in the gospel assurance that "even the hairs of your head are all counted" (Matt 10:30). We detect it as well in what follows in this, Jesus' second Matthean, discourse:

> "So do not be afraid; you are of more value than many sparrows. Everyone therefore who acknowledges me before others, I also will acknowledge before my Father in heaven; but whoever denies me before others, I also will deny before my Father in heaven. Do not think that I have come to bring peace to the earth; I have not come to bring peace, but a sword. For I have come to set a man against his father, and a daughter against her mother, and a daughter-in-law against her mother-in-law; and one's foes will be members of one's own household. Whoever loves father or mother more than me is not worthy of me; and whoever loves son or daughter more than me is not worthy of me; and whoever does not take up the cross and follow me is not worthy of me. Those who find their life will lose it, and those who lose their life for my sake will find it." (Matt 10:31–39)

---

6. Kierkegaard, *Point of View*, 10.

Yet in placing due emphasis on, and directly addressing the single individual, we must not be misinterpreted as supporting the inherently selfish, secular cult of individualism. The second commandment that is like the first and greatest admonishes us: "You shall love your neighbor as yourself" (Lev 18:19; Matt 22:39). Elsewhere, we read: "Do nothing from selfish ambition or conceit, but in humility regard others as *better than* yourselves" (Phil 2:3). In dialectical juxtaposition to the aformentioned passage in which Jesus brings a sword to separate the individual from the often oppressive bonds of familial idolatry, we find this important passage:

> Then (Jesus) said to them, "You have a fine way of rejecting the commandment of God in order to keep your tradition! For Moses said, 'Honor your father and your mother'; and, 'Whoever speaks evil of father or mother must surely die.' But you say that if anyone tells father or mother, 'Whatever support you might have had from me is Corban' (that is, an offering to God)—then you no longer permit doing anything for a father or mother, thus making void the word of God through your tradition that you have handed on. And you do many things like this." (Mark 7:9–13)

Again, let us allow Kierkegaard to remind us emphatically of the uniquely high view Christianity holds of the individual. It is paganism, he says, that regards the human race as higher than the single individual. But Christianity reverses this. The Christian faith regards the single individual Christian believer as higher than the crowd, higher than the rabble. How can he say this? Recall that the crowd lives in the esthetic realm and the believer, as such, will have made the leap of faith. Such a leap is *inseparable* from true repentance. Therefore, we are told, from the standpoint of faith, that is, in the eyes of heaven, "there will be more joy in heaven over one sinner who repents than over ninety-nine righteous persons who need no repentance" (Luke 15:7, 10). Clearly, Christian preaching must learn anew, or perhaps for the first time, to uphold the importance of the single individual in the eyes of God in such a way that does not, wittingly or unwittingly, grant a false warrant to the secular cult of individualism.

Here again, we find how thoroughly ill-equipped is hermeneutics to the task, which demands attention to particularity and diversity, but which ever fails to arrive at particularity's ultimate *locus*, the single individual. Instead, it quickly hides the individual in "the crowd," in "identity politics," in "affinity groups," in "advocacy groups." This it does by addressing particularity only at the societal, cultural, group, and subgroup level. That hermeneutics piously acknowledges one subgroup after another does not render its categorizations any more righteous. Hermeneutics is thus hypocritical in the extreme in that it lacks the hyper-self-criticism it enjoins on every other discipline. Disallowing any discussion of, for instance, the universals scripture attributes to the individual and to human experience, universals such as mortality and sin, hermeneutics admits nothing of either individual diversity or a common humanity. In this sense, hermeneutics is unable to uphold either pole of this important dialectic. Indeed, it lacks the leverage to do so, since it stands at such a far remove from faith, that is, it operates predominantly within the esthetic sphere, and when it aspires to something higher, it is able to conceive of nothing higher than ethics.

One of the most important texts for reclaiming the true content of Christian preaching, however, also serves as the needed dialectical corrective to this sorely needed affirmation of God's love for the single individual, and thus guards it against the heresy of the Free Spirit, that is, against selfish individualism. With Peter's identification of Jesus (in a manner inclusive of both Hebrew and Greek thought) as "the Messiah, the Son of the Living God," we learn that we are to expect this very proclamation, this clearest, purest, most unambiguous, attributive core of Christian preaching, to result in the foundation of the church (Matt 16:13–20).

Further, this proclamation is to be heard as the clear, divinely inspired corrective to the yeast, the false teaching, of the Pharisees and Sadducees (Matt 16:6‾12), which the disciples, who did not yet understand themselves as church, as the body of Christ, as bread for the world, mistakenly took as a reference to the temporal bread which they forgot to take along with them in their boat, the vessel which became yet another symbol of the church and its mission.

Thus, we see this *individual/ecclesial* dialectic in the manner in which Jesus sometimes addressed himself to the individual and sometimes to the crowd; sometimes reveals himself in risen form to the individual, e.g., to Cephas (1 Cor 15:5a), James (15:7a), or Mary Magdalene; sometimes to the twelve (15:5b); sometimes to five hundred disciples at one time (15:6); sometimes to two weary disciples in Emmaus (Luke 24:13ff.). Perhaps most significantly, the risen and glorified Lord sometimes reveals himself to a gathering, yet in the midst of that very gathering, does so in a special way to the single individual: to Paul, amidst his fellow travelers, who heard the voice but did not see the light, on the road to Damascus (Acts 9:1–9); to Thomas in the upper room (John 20:24–29), etc.

We see this dialectic as well in apparently mundane grammatical fashion in Paul's varied use of the singular and plural forms of the second person pronoun, *su* and *'umeis*. Perhaps the most vivid representation of this dialectic, however, may be seen liturgically in the sacramental life of the church. In the Sacrament of the Lord's Supper, believers are admonished to discern the body and wait for one another (1 Cor 11:29–33), yet they are fed individually from the common loaf and drink from the common cup of salvation. Even more explicitly, in the rite of initiation, the individual candidate is *baptized by name* (with no mention of the familial or "group" surname) *into the church*. The Reformation rightly proscribed the private conduct of the sacraments and successfully reclaimed them as church rites. Yet in neither case is God's loving provision for the individual lost or obscured.

Preaching must likewise rigorously maintain this dialectic. To this end, preachers must recognize the tensions that develop between the ecclesial model that emphasizes individual transformation and that which stresses socialization into the family of faith. The tension exists in every church, but few churches manage to avoid some form of bias or imbalance. While it is generally easy to determine the model that is operative in any given congregation, rare is the pastor who recognizes that both models must be operative in every congregation and who seeks to maintain this dialectic with careful intentionality.

While it is true that congregations which operate with extreme emphasis on socialization die a long, slow death for lack of any renewal or transformation, it is equally true, and somewhat ironic that, when congregations which exclusively emphasize personal transformation finally split off from their lifeless denominations, the first things they do is create a socialization structure, including a building with a state-of-the-art nursery!

§2.2 The Indwelling/Indwelt Dialectic: Clothed in Christ in You

Our earlier reference to the sacraments serves as a helpful analogue to the *second* dialectic to be maintained in our preaching of the kingdom. Here it helps to recall that according to Karl Barth, the proclamation of the Word is defined as preaching and the sacraments. The sacraments understood as the visible Word can assist us in amending our preaching the audible Word so that we maintain both the sense in which, *in faith*, we indwell Christ and are indwelt by him through the Holy Spirit. What is most visible in baptism, if not the external washing with water? What is most visible in the Lord's Supper, if not the ingesting, the internalizing, the eating and drinking of bread and wine, the body and blood of Christ? As Jesus said in one of his many disputations with the Jews: "Those who eat my flesh and drink my blood abide in me, and I in them" (John 6:56).

Clearly the sacraments involve much more than meets the eye. Many other visible and invisible aspects, many other internal and external movements, may also be discerned. Foremost among the visible features is, of course, the church itself, the all encompassing "womb" of the church, seen in font, architecture, and especially, the gathered people. So it is with the Lord's Supper. As previously mentioned, it is imperative that we discern "the body," by which is meant not only the common loaf and our sense that the celebrant acts as a stand-in for Christ, but once again and most importantly, the gathered people. This is neither the place to thoroughly develop a sacramental theology, nor even to attempt a sketch thereof. It is enough to simply remark that the visible form of the invisible grace we know in the sacraments is a visual enactment of the same dialectic to which preaching must also attend.

As with the frequently observable imbalance between personal transformation and communal socialization, here we find that preachers who emphasize the former tend to speak almost exclusively (though with insufficient attention to grammatical number) of "Christ in you (pl.), the hope of glory" (Col 1:27) and of Paul's assertion that "*your* (pl.) *body* (sg., but several variant mss. use the pl.) is a temple of the Holy Spirit within you" (1 Cor 6:19). Would that such individualistic readings would attend to the remainder of the verse, which deems the body as that "which you have from God," and reminds the listener that you (pl.) are not your own."

We do not have the luxury, however, of returning to the question of the dialectic between the singular individual with the plurality of the congregation. Rather, what is important to recognize here is that, *in faith*, we have the benefits of the presence of Christ and the Holy Spirit operating *within and without us, inside and all about* us. The clearest expressions of this dialectic are found in Jesus' farewell discourse in the Gospel of John, where our Lord tells the disciples, regarding the time when the world will no longer see him, though the disciples themselves will see him: "On that day you will know that I am in my Father, and *you in me, and I in you*" (John 14:20). In Jesus' reply to Judas (not Iscariot), we are told: "Those who love me will keep my word, and my Father will love them, and we will come to them and make our home with them" (John 14:23). Further, in each of four consecutive verses of John 15, the disciples are to understand their relation to the true vine as a mutual indwelling.

"Abide in me as I abide in you. Just as the branch cannot bear fruit by itself unless it abides in the vine, neither can you unless you abide in me. I am the vine, you are the branches. *Those who abide in me and I in them bear much fruit,* because apart from me you can do nothing. Whoever does not abide in me is thrown away like a branch and withers; such branches are gathered, thrown into the fire, and burned. If you abide in me, and my words abide in you, ask for whatever you wish, and it will be done for you" (John 15:4–7). Later, Jesus prays, regarding the disciples, "As you, Father, are in me and I am in you, *may they also be in us,* so that the world may believe that you have sent me" (John 17:21).

It must be said, however, that the New Testament witness places a far greater emphasis on the believer and the church abiding *in Christ* than the popular emphasis in North American Christianity on *the Christ in you* would indicate. Clearly there is good reason for this, for as we have seen faith plays a doubly dialectical function, that is, we can say that one is *in faith,* both in dialectical opposition to *sin* and within the sphere of faith itself, when we speak of the sense in which we are *in Christ,* that is, enjoying his external benefits.

But let us demarcate the boundaries of this dialectic of mutual indwelling for faith by noting the nature of our frequent errors. Preaching which aims primarily at *transformation,* to the extent that it takes account of Christian life *in Christ,* frequently interprets these external benefits as having more to do with the protective armor of God (Eph 6) than with the blessed communion of the saints and the reality of fellowship in the kingdom of heaven. Preaching which aims primarily at *socialization,* however, easily confuses the church itself, the body of Christ, with the person of Christ, to the extent that Christ's headship is, as far as de facto church leaders are concerned and for all practical purposes, decapitated. Rather than letting "the same mind be in you that was in Christ Jesus" (Phil 2:5‑11), socialization models of ecclesiology replace the mind of Christ with the collective wisdom of the privilege occupants of hierarchical positions. Thus, the overly socialized church has no provision for the occasion when "the LORD has put a lying spirit in the mouth of these your prophets" (2 Chr 18:11‑22).

By contrast, preaching that emphasizes exclusively internal benefits of *the Christ in you,* or more popularly, the affective affirmation of *"Jesus in my heart,"* can only do so at the expense of the largest part of the New Testament, with its countless, though easily overlooked, references to our being *in Christ, in faith, as members of his body.* Such one-sided emphasis on the indwelling Christ carries with it the (admittedly naive) implication that Christ must be smaller than the human body in order to "fit inside." The result is a disastrously reduced understanding of Christ. Here the ecclesial view serves as the needed corrective, which reminds us that we are not only to be clothed in Christ (Rom 13:13⁻14), but it is equally true that "in him we live and move and have our being" (Acts 17:28).

In the history of the Christian church, there is perhaps no better expression of this dialectic than in the prayer known as St. Patrick's breastplate.

> *Christ be with me, Christ within me.*
> *Christ behind me, Christ before me,*
> *Christ beside me, Christ to win me,*
> *Christ to comfort and restore me.*
> *Christ beneath me, Christ above me,*
> *Christ in quiet, Christ in danger,*
> *Christ in the hearts of all who love me,*
> *Christ in the mouth of friend and stranger.*

Much, much farther back in the church's memory, however, is the story of Noah, whose ark, like the disciples' boat we mentioned earlier, has come to serve as a type of the church and its mission (cf. Acts 27–28). Before we conclude our all-too-brief treatment of this important dialectic between indwelling Christ and being indwelt by him, it is worth recalling God's explicit instruction to Noah in the construction of the ark: "Make yourself an ark of cypress wood; make rooms in the ark, and *cover it inside and out* with pitch." (Gen 6:14)

§2.3 Analogy and Dialectic, Metaphor and Paradox, Parable and Disputation: Set Your Mind on Things That Are Above!

The final dialectic to be considered strictly *from the standpoint of faith,* by which we understand ourselves to be overtaken by the leading edge (so to speak) of the coming eschaton, pertains to biblical interpretation generally, and involves analogy and dialectic itself, that is, dialectic in the *contradictory* sense. The tension between analogy and dialectic, however, is but one way in which the positive, associative and the negative, dissociative movements of interpretation are made. On the positive side, we find frequent references in theological (and so-called hermeneutical) literature to similitude, analogy, the metaphorical *is,* and parable, which often begins as similitude: "The kingdom of heaven is like . . ." On the negative side of interpretation, every analogy meets with a corrective, contradictory dialectic, every metaphor carries with it an *is not*, every parable, if it does not execute a surprising reversal, seems to be juxtaposed with, or even embedded within, a dialectical disputation. The preacher should not allow the variations in terminology or the shades of technical differences between the terms to obscure the fact that *faithful interpretation will always attend to these two general movements*: positive and negative, constructive and critical, associative and dissociative.

While hermeneutical literature abounds which treats of these dynamics, it is urgent and critical for the preacher to recognize that biblical interpretation from the standpoint of faith is a "wholly other" enterprise than hermeneutics, one that, *through prayer*, relies solely on the Holy Spirit as both scripture's author and interpretive instructor, not on human wisdom or a spirit by any other name, (1) to make the needed definitive associations (e.g., Jesus is the Lamb of God who takes away the sins of the world and the High Priest in the order of Melchizedek), *and* (2) to make the needed dissociative moves that negate every atheological, anti-Christian, or heretical misinterpretation, ranging from the literalistic quip that Jesus was no four-footed woolly animal to the hermeneutical objection that atonement Christology is too historically contextual and culturally conditioned to bear any significance for enlightened modern people.[7] Preaching must be able to say what is true in light of scripture and according to the reminding of the Spirit, and what is obviously *not* true due to a clear departure from scripture and a lack of conformity to the Spirit's teaching.

This third dialectical tension between interpretation's paradoxes, however, must ultimately lead us, by means of the Spirit (as divine reminder, as witness to Christ, as the "third" person of the Trinity), from the Word of God written to "the absolute paradox," to the Incarnate Word of God, Christ Jesus, the God-man himself. Christian interpretation of scripture is and must remain Christocentric interpretation, that is, it must maintain the distinction between God's means of authoritative revelation through scripture and the revealed God whom we know in Christ Jesus.

---

7. On the need for fresh interpretation of the doctrine of the Atonement and the need for preaching the cross, see Brown's excellent book, *Cross Talk*.

"I write to you, not because you do not know the truth, but because you know it, and you know that no lie comes from the truth. Who is the liar but the one who denies that Jesus is the Christ? This is the antichrist, the one who denies the Father and the Son. No one who denies the Son has the Father; everyone who confesses the Son has the Father also. Let what you heard from the beginning abide in you. If what you heard from the beginning abides in you, then you will abide in the Son and in the Father. And this is what he has promised us, eternal life. / I write these things to you concerning those who would deceive you. As for you, the anointing that you received from him abides in you, and so you do not need anyone to teach you. But as his anointing teaches you about all things, and is true and is not a lie, and just as it has taught you, abide in him." (1 John 2:21–27)

§3. The True Content of Christian Preaching: Christ Jesus is the Narrow Way

Nevertheless, it is not as though faithful interpretation involves our simple and direct relocation from the esthetic sphere to that of faith, our casual crossing of a plane or a line or a membrane that separates the two spheres of the old and new creations respectively, the kingdom of the world and the kingdom of heaven. The kingdom of heaven recognizes no earthly passport or permit. The only such mark we bear is that of baptism. The only such seal we possess is that of the Spirit. But baptism, and the seal of the Spirit with which it is accompanied, derive from a specific person and a specific point. "There is one body and one Spirit, just as you were called to the one hope of your calling, one Lord, one faith, one baptism, one God and Father of all, who is above all and through all and in all" (Eph 4:4–6). No, the one faith, the one baptism, must first be understood as the most precise and particular *point*, before it can open out into the heavenly realm, the *sphere* of faith. In the person and the work of Christ, the leading edge of the coming kingdom has come! But it has come with his baptism by John in the Jordan "to fulfill all righteousness" (Matt 3:15), the one and only baptism, which Jesus (Mark 10:31–40) clearly yet paradoxically links with his crucifixion between two bandits (Matt 27: 38; Mark 15:27; Luke 23:33). No, we cannot casually cross from one kingdom to another (Mark 10:24–25). We must pass by way of, even *through*, the most impossibly tiny and terrible point, which should rightly produce in us great angst, *anfechtungen,* "fear and trembling," for it is described in scripture as "the narrow gate" [Gk: *tes stenes pules*; L: *angustam portam*] (Matt 7:13), which can only be the cross of Christ. Therefore, our third *point* (!) of consideration will understand Christology itself, or more precisely, Christ Jesus himself, as *the person in and with whom alone* and *the point at which* the kingdom of heaven meets this present age. Is it not of this eschatological rendezvous in Christ that the psalmist once sang: "Steadfast love and faithfulness will meet; righteousness and peace will kiss each other" (Ps 85:10)?

"But in fact Christ has been raised from the dead, the first fruits of those who have died. For since death came through a human being, the resurrection of the dead has also come through a human being; for as all die in Adam, so all will be made alive in Christ. But each in his own order: Christ the first fruits, then at his coming those who belong to Christ" (1 Cor 15:20-23; cf. Rev 1:4b-5a). In other words, the coming age has already *begun* to come, at the most singular, particular point. Note that we must avoid "upsetting the faith of some" with the gangrenous talk of "Hymenaeus and Philetus, who have swerved from the truth by claiming that the resurrection has already taken place" (2 Tim 2:17-18). On the other hand, will faithful interpretation by the Spirit allow us to thoughtlessly and blindly dismiss Paul's assertion that "the present form of this world is passing away" (1 Cor 7:31) as though he were simply wrong? Must we not first make the leap of faith and acknowledge that, though we may not understand it yet, there is divine truth to be learned here? And even if we were so crass and foolish to do so, would we not be even more foolish to pretend that his claim, that "salvation is nearer to us now than when we became believers" (Rom 13:11), is not all the more urgent for us today? Can we really convince ourselves that the apostle was simply wrong to declare in his day that "the appointed time has grown short" (1 Cor 7:29), and live as though it has not meanwhile grown two millenia shorter? Surely, if we have anything approaching a faithful epistemology, we can only "regard the patience of our Lord as salvation" (2 Pet 3:15).

§3.1 Repentance Is Believing the Gospel: The All-Inclusive Divestiture

The vertical and horizontal beams of the cross present us with a point of spatio-temporal convergence, a uniquely unique divine-human person, a God-man, who is himself the pioneer and perfecter of our faith (Heb 12:2), indeed, the *one Lord* who *is* our *one faith.* Christ *is* our faith? Is this hyperbole? By no means! The interpretive arithmetic is so simple a child can do it (Matt 11:25; Luke 10:21). When in the gospel narratives *Jesus* heals, forgives, and saves someone, he says, "*Your faith* has saved you." How then can the preacher preach rightly who fails to see that the saving Christ Jesus *is* our faith, our righteousness, our justification, our salvation? So we allow ourselves to be guided by this most basic Christian proclamation: "Jesus is Lord, the Christ, the Son of the Living God!" This is the true test of all *faithful* preaching (Matt 16:15–19), the evidence, despite all other appearances, that the Holy Spirit is present with the speaker and present in the speech, for "no one speaking by the Spirit of God ever says 'Let Jesus be cursed!' and no one can say 'Jesus is Lord' except by the Holy Spirit" (1 Cor 12:3).

So too are we to understand the outgrowth of Jesus' own preaching of the kingdom of God (Mark 1:14–15) from John's preaching "a baptism of repentance for the forgiveness of sins" (Mark 1:4). The fact that the gospels were written in Greek cannot hide the definitive Hebrew parallelism in Jesus' first words in the earliest gospel. "Now after John was arrested, Jesus came to Galilee, proclaiming the good news of God, and saying, 'The time is fulfilled, and the kingdom of God has come near; repent, and believe in the good news'" (Mark 1:14–15). Surely we are to understand that "the time is fulfilled" *means* "the kingdom of God has come near." Likewise, "to repent" *means* "to believe in the good news." The coming of the leading edge of the coming kingdom in the person, the work, the baptism, and the preaching of Christ Jesus is the only available and only requisite "point of contact" with the eschatological sphere of faith. This eschaton *is* the one hope. This faith *is* the one baptism of repentance, defined as believing the good news. This baptism *is* the cross of the one Lord in whose one body and one Spirit we become participants through the one faith. With this Reformed reminder of *sola Christus, sola fides,* we must enter the task of preaching by the same gate through which *sola Sanctus Spiritus* (we pray and hope and trust) will use our preaching to usher our listeners into the kingdom, that is, through the narrow way, the way of the cross.

But herein lies the problem of preaching, namely, the impossibility of it apart from the God for whom all things are possible (Matt 19:26; Mark 10:27). The nature of this impossibility is that we must enter through the narrow gate, the eye of a needle so narrow, in fact, that *even one at a time* we cannot wriggle through on our own. Thus, we speak *first* of the undeniable dialectic of divestiture, of putting off the old, which is the inescapable dialectical *result* of the "belief-ful" repentance and forgiveness of sins that are to be proclaimed *inclusively* to one and all.

> "And you who were once estranged and hostile in mind, doing evil deeds, he has now reconciled in his fleshly body through death, so as to present you holy and blameless and irreproachable before him— *provided that you continue securely established and steadfast in the faith, without shifting from the hope promised by the gospel that you heard, which has been proclaimed to every creature under heaven.*" (Col 1:21–23a). "Then I saw another angel flying in midheaven, with *an eternal gospel to proclaim to those who live on the earth—to every nation and tribe and language and people*" (Rev 14:6).

The Word of God calls everyone inclusively to the repentance of faith. And when we respond, we find that something is indeed jettisoned in turning our attention to and embarking upon the narrow path that lies before us. To seek the face of God (Ps 27:8) is to seek God's face first revealed in the Word who became flesh and was crucified, to consider oneself one among the "all" *[pantas]* that he draws to himself *[elkuso]* as he is lifted up on the cross (John 12:32). This being drawn is your summons to faith. It is, at the same time, the call of the Spirit speaking through the apostles to flee from idols (1 Cor 10:14; 1 John 5:21). It is the moment for the renunciation of the former, worldly ways of the flesh. Therefore, preaching will not apologize for or hide the fact that *all* are called to repent and believe the good news. In short, inclusivity *will* characterize much of our rhetoric, even as narrowness and exclusivity will be a legitimate function of our epistemology, our interpretation, and our proclamation, all of which are required to maintain a Christocentric focus. Nevertheless, inclusion and exclusion do not, properly speaking, constitute the dialectic at issue, unless we are to raise soteriology to a level of importance that Calvin for one would not give it. Rather, since salvation is the byproduct of faith, and faith must always be faith in something, and faith is Truth, saving faith is only ever faith in Christ Jesus the Truth (John 14:6), the needed dialectic is one that does not ask whether the human subject is saved or damned, included or excluded. No, the necessary dialectic is one that keeps its eyes fixed upon the God-man as the atoning sacrifice for sin, and thus, as the narrow way for saving faith.

§3.2 Either Faith or Offense: The All-Sufficient Atonement

Because we understand the call to repentance as the all-inclusive summons to believe the good news, that is, that gospel proclamation for *"every nation and tribe and language and people"* (Rev 14:6), we must also recognize the fact that the provision which Christ Jesus has made by his grace through his death upon the cross is *all-sufficient* (2 Cor 12:9), in that it has provided for us the needed entry way *through* the narrow straits of his suffering *into* the kingdom of heaven. Christ's perfect, once-for-all ransom (for sin and for the innumerable specific sins attributable to every sinner, to the church, and to the world) has opened the way. Here we see again that the person of Christ Jesus himself is all-sufficient, that "in him all things hold together" (Col 1:17), since, at one and the same time, this divine-human person *is* the Way (John 14:6), the sheepgate (John 10:7–9), and he fully *contains* the way, "the new and living way that he opened for us through the curtain (that is, through his flesh)" (Heb 10:20). The gospel itself, inherently all-inclusive, we proclaim openly and unashamedly, denying any false doctrine that would imply God is somehow stingy with grace, denying as well any false doctrine that would limit God's freedom apart from any freely chosen self-limitation that is in accordance with the divine will and purpose, with God's decision to enter into and keep covenant, and further, denying any human teaching which presumes to know better than God what is required to put an end to sin and to secure our salvation.

Yet we will also recognize that many are in fact offended by this doctrine we preach and may choose and, in fact, many have chosen, to exclude themselves from the eternal freedom from sin and its eternal consequences that Christ, by his atoning work, has purchased for them. This is the undeniably and unavoidably *exclusive* element in Christianity, what Kierkegaard termed "the possibility of offense." Nevertheless, this exclusiveness may not and must not be attributed to the doctrine itself. No, it is only ever attributable to and is the full responsibility of the one who excludes himself or herself by taking offense at the gospel. The risk of offense is not a possibility that preachers must seek to avoid. No, false preaching may indeed erect unnecessary, exclusivistic, or legalistic stumbling blocks and woe to the legalist who sets them up.

> "Woe to you lawyers! For you have taken away the key of knowledge; you did not enter yourselves, and you hindered those who

were entering" (Luke 11:52). "It would be better for you if a mill-
stone were hung around your neck and you were thrown into
the sea than for you to cause one of these little ones to stumble"
(Luke 17:2).

But the true preacher will neither be daunted by the charge that
the preaching of Christ crucified is too exclusive, nor seek therefore
to preach a different gospel (Gal 1:8) or change the doctrine or herald
a broader, easier way to heaven than the one which God alone is able
to provide and has in fact provided in Christ. No, Jesus himself said,
"Enter through the narrow gate; for the gate is wide and the road is
easy that leads to destruction, and there are many who take it. For the
gate is narrow and the road is hard that leads to life, and there are few
who find it" (Matt 7:13–14). The preacher who is true to this word will
present Christ as the Way, the Narrow Way, and leave the response, either *faith* or *offense*, gratitude or grief, inclusion or exclusion, up to the
listener as she encounters the Living Word as the Crucified One and
the Holy Spirit as the Spirit of Truth. The faithful preacher will neither reduce God's ideal requirements (Calvin's first use of the law), nor
change God's unchangeable and unchanging Word. The preacher will
preach *this* Word and, God willing, *people* will be changed, transformed
by faith, recreated by the Spirit, renewed in Christ.

> "Everyone who calls on the name of the Lord shall be saved."
> But how are they to call on one in whom they have not believed?
> And how are they to believe in one of whom they have never
> heard? And how are they to hear without someone to proclaim
> him? And how are they to proclaim him unless they are sent?
> (Rom 10:13‾15).

§3.3 Historical Singularity and Contemporaneous Ubiquity: The Cruciform Truth

Finally and decisively, we arrive at the cross itself, at the Crucified One
himself: the true content of Christian preaching. He is the God-man, and
viewed objectively, he is absolutely paradoxical. He is the (Narrow) Way,
the (Paradoxical) Truth, the (Faithful) Life. We call him the God-man
not to flaunt his maleness, but so that we will not forget his uniquely
unique, absolutely singular, historical particularity: a Jew, born of a willing woman named Mary, born of the tribe of Judah, circumcised on the

eighth day. But neither will we embark on historical and hermeneutical quests for him, as though he were not everywhere available as the real spiritual presence of God in our contemporary situation: the Living Word, the Son of God, conceived and anointed by the Holy Spirit. No, as the crucified, risen, ascended Christ, we know him in contemporaneity as our intercessor and mediator, who is "near," who "will come again," and indeed, is "coming soon." It is before him, who was lifted up on the cross, it is before him at his singular *locus*, his unique spatio-temporal *point*, the point at which he was pierced, hands and feet, head and side, for you, for me, for us, and for everyone who would hear and accept him, that we face the ultimate dialectic of existential crisis at *every* point in *our* lives, that is, the existential outworking in fear and trembling of the eschatological dialectic between our indwelling Christ (our common baptism into and with him) and our being indwelt by him. Here the same tension exists between his substitution on our behalf and our participation in his sufferings, his humiliation, his vindication, his transfiguration.

In the esthetic sphere, in the Johannine world, in the present age, we may perhaps have known of Christ, but there we regarded him from afar; our contemplatation of his form was unappreciative and unresponsive: "he had no form or majesty that we should look at him, nothing in his appearance that we should desire him" (Isa 53:2). We may have conceded that he led a beautiful life, had a beautiful mind, or at best, admitted that he was a great moral teacher, perhaps even the greatest. Here, however, at the point of entry, at the narrow gate of his suffering because of my sin and yours, the revelation of his true identity is apparent in its most pathetic, critical form, its *cruci*-form, whereas in the *eschaton*, the form with which we are (or will be) concerned is the *imitation* of Christ as our *prototype*, the worship of God in spirit and in truth. Thus, we recall, once again, that the difference between *esthetics* as *imitation and poesis* in the present age and the *transformed esthes*, the robe of righteous *ethics* and good deeds with which we are clothed in the *eschaton*, in the age to come, is that the former, for all its tasteful discriminations among a pantheon of forms and objects, does *not* see or believe that the Christ "is the image of the invisible God" (Col 1:15) and still less does it recognize that he alone is worthy of human *imitation, poesis*, and *praise*. But the faithful preacher of the gospel is another creature entirely, a new creation, a servant who is divinely called not to speak on his or her own, but one who under the guidance of the Word and the Spirit refers everything and everyone to the Cruciform Truth, through the Narrow Way, Christ Jesus our Savior and Living, Loving Lord, the true content of Christian proclamation.

§4. The Definition of Preaching According to a Penitential Homiletic

What then is preaching? Elsewhere I have advanced ten normative criteria for what may be called a penitential homiletic, one that aspires to faithfulness and love, to love with faith (Eph 6:23), to faith working through love (Gal 5:6).[8] Here I would venture to add that such a homiletic, conceived under the pressure of the sort of dialectical interpretation we have set forth above, would define preaching as follows. *Preaching is divinely authored and authorized human speech that lifts up and proclaims Christ crucified, the uniquely unique God-man, who, because he is risen, ascended, and seated at the right hand of power, and because he, who is coming quickly and is even now contemporaneous with, available to, concerned for, and loves every creature and is desirous that every human being should come to repentance and become a new creation in him, will in conjunction with this human speech, draw all to himself, for "there is salvation in no one else."* What the God-man will do with and for each creature once drawn is entirely up to him, but to those who are received into and remain in his new covenant of faith he gives ample assurances of eternal peace and rest, life and love, fellowship and joy. It is in the service of this good news that the human preacher, continually subject to the ongoing work of the Holy Spirit, prayerfully seeks to be faithful, and realizes this faithfulness through continual leaps of faith, works of love, and acts of repentance.

---

8. See my Introduction above, and "Penitential Homiletic," 350–58.

4

Two Sermons on the Narrow Gate

§1. "Enter through the Narrow Gate"[1]
(Psalm 66; Matthew 7:13–14)

PRAYER
"O you who dwell in the heavens,"
you who, in a garden,
first revealed yourself as risen from the tomb:
"my companions are listening for your voice; let me hear it,"
for you are the Beloved of God. Amen.

Jesus said, "Enter through the narrow gate; for the gate is wide and the road is easy that leads to destruction, and there are many who take it. For the gate is narrow and the road is hard that leads to life, and there are few who find it." (Matthew 7:13–14)

I can think of a lot of reasons *not* to preach this word:

First, this is not an Easter text, as such. It seems more like a Lenten text, I suppose, as it urges us to seek the hard road; but we have emerged from the austerity of Lent into the broad space of Easter. No, this is not an Easter text.

Second, the gate of which Jesus speaks, the narrow gate, is the gate of *distress* (Rom 8:35); a *crushing* gate (2 Cor 4:8); a path of *hard-*

---

1. Preached on Thursday, April 12, 2007, Miller Chapel, Princeton Theological Seminary; and Tuesday, April 14, 2008, Blades Chapel, University of Dubuque Theological Seminary, IA.

ship (6:4) and even *calamity* (12:10); it is a *restrictive* (6:12) entrance; the Vulgate renders this adjective *angustos*; in which you can hear the German: *angst*. I confess, none of these attributes play well in the mind of a claustrophobic asthmatic with a softening waistline. Neither is the idea of restricted access likely to meet with a warm reception in the seminaries of a denomination that has recently committed itself to the study and promotion of "full inclusion of people with disabilities." My late father, an architect, was always a strong advocate for what was then called "handicapped access," so it goes against the grain of many deeply-held convictions to entertain a plain-sense reading of this saying of Jesus. Neither will such a commendation of narrowness meet with cheers from folks who have rightly vowed to learn the hard lessons of history, to repent of past injustices, especially the tendency to allow the church of Jesus Christ to lose the distinctiveness by which it may be clearly distinguished from an *exclusive* country club.

Third, to speak positively of the narrow gate, or of anything at all that is *narrow*, is, in these contentious days, to risk being taken as intellectually, socially, culturally, or in some other way, "narrow-minded," to risk being misheard and misunderstood as somehow suggesting that a certain general restrictiveness or conservatism (*with respect to everything*) is good.

As in everything, our verbs, our stances, our postures, our claims demand, at every point, the proper objects and qualifiers. "*With what* should we be liberal and generous? *What* are those things that we must learn to conserve?" Just as Paul chided the Corinthians, for example, for *narrowing their affections* (2 Cor 6:12); just as Jesus taught us to *love with unrestricted love*, we can no more justify a so-called conservative position if it causes or allows the love of many to grow cold, . . . we can no more do that than we can justify a liberal and widespread substitution of love's shabby impostor: "tolerance," for love itself. (How many people do you know who, when it comes right down to it, long to be tolerated, rather than loved? Not very many, I expect.) No, the Great Commandment is "you shall love," not "you shall tolerate."

Fourth, to risk a generalization, we—and by *we* I mean people who study, teach in, or otherwise frequent institutions of theological inquiry—we are a people who like to keep our options open; seminary is an exploratory time and place; it is a mercy, indeed, a luxury, if you will; a sabbatical time-out to ride the theological merry-go-round, plunge down the most compelling avenues of ministry; and imagine a world of countless possibilities for discipleship, service, growth and witness. Yet, with startling suddenness, the springtime of senior year is upon some of you, and what should appear as the springing forth of new life is accompanied and tinged by an untimely, and perhaps unwelcome, autumnal dropping of many leaves from the possibility tree. The realization strikes home that, of all your imagined calls, only one will be the best fit, for now anyway; of all the doors that may be opened to you, there is only one through which you may pass, or at least only one at a time; and if you came single to seminary, of all your imagined partners, there may be only one, or perhaps no one at all, going where the Lord is calling *you* to go.

> Enter through the narrow gate; ... For the gate is narrow and the
> road is hard that leads to life, and there are few who find it.

Given more time, I expect we could come up with a sufficiently towering, terrifying list of reasons to scare ourselves away from the narrow gate altogether. Off-putting as it is, however, there is a lot at stake in this imperative. In Luke's gospel, Jesus speaks of the narrow gate in response to the explicitly *soteriological* question: "Lord, will only a few be saved?" (13:23), and Jesus' reply comes with the further disconcerting detail that, "many ... will *try* to enter and will not be able" (13:24).

The narrow gate, in many ways, constitutes a worrisome word, despite the fact that Paul says, "do not worry about anything" (Phil 4:6); despite the fact that Jesus speaks of the narrow gate directly after warning us: "do not worry about your life, what you will eat or what you will drink, or about your body, what you will wear" (Matt 6:24); "do not worry about tomorrow, for tomorrow will bring worries of its own" (6:34). But more worrisome still is the risk of *not* preaching the narrow gate: "for the gate is wide and the road is easy that leads to *destruction*, and there are *many* who take it."

The stakes are high; higher even than discerning the right call, the right car, the right house, the right spouse. No, the Bible does not commend narrow-mindedness; neither does Doctor Seuss; but it *does* urge us to be *single*-minded. As Brother Søren said, "purity of heart is to will *one thing*, to will the good in truth." One *cannot* single-mindedly will to sin, because sin and evil are by definition double-mindedness, they are behind every attempt to serve *Both* God *And* Mammon. Thus, the *Either/Or*; thus, the task of doing Christian theology in a pluralistic world is (as I see it) to single-mindedly think dialectically, or to dialectically think, act, and speak with the mind of Christ. Is *that* not a *narrow* gate? The single-mindedness we are to seek is none other than "the mind of Christ" (1 Cor 2:16), the mind of him who urges us to "strive first for the kingdom of God and his righteousness, and all these [other] things [that God knows you need] will be given to you as well" (Matt 6:33), and who adds: "and when you find the kingdom, the gate you are looking for is the narrow one, the harrowing, scary, distressing one; yes, *that* is the one that leads to life."

Yes, we can think of a lot of reasons *not* to preach this word concerning the narrow gate. But the easiest, yes, the *easiest* reason of all is that this is neither an Easter text, nor a Lenten text, nor an Advent text, nor a Christmas text; believe it or not, it does not even appear in Ordinary Time. The fact is that the narrow gate as such is not mentioned at all, either in its Matthean or its Lukan dress, in the *Revised Common Lectionary*; and it is easy to as pie to go round and round the calendar, to go round and round Years A, B, and C, to preach the gospel lections from Matthew and Luke, year after year, and never once warn your flock about the broad way, the easy way, that leads to destruction; it is as easy as, . . . well, as easy as the way that leads to destruction (!) to never once inform your listeners that it is the *narrow* way that leads to life, to never once admonish them to seek it.

I cannot explain this strange omission from the lectionary, though I expect the reasons we have listed for avoiding it will come close. Perhaps some think it is possible to widen the door to the kingdom of God by narrowing the functional canon of the church. Perhaps like Detroit, some are so married to the fossil fuel of inclusive/exclusive thinking that we cannot imagine how the alternative dialectic of the narrow way that leads to God's wide mercy can ever empower our preaching. Perhaps some fear the opinions of those who measure the broadness or narrowness of the mind of Christ according to their own skewed balances of judgment. Perhaps some fear having their options reduced, thinned, or narrowed down to one and only one "way" to life: as when Jesus says: "I am the Way" (John 14:6). But the saying stands, the narrow way beckons, neglected and overgrown as he may appear, like the door to the Secret Garden; and in the end, the stakes are far too high not to preach it!

This then is the good news that transcends all our worry, namely, that the narrow gate is more familiar than we may realize; that our crucified and risen Lord *is* himself the Narrow Way; the "sheep gate," as he says in John's gospel; the Good Shepherd who calls each by name; it is Christ, the Beloved of God, not our *Book(s) of Order* and *Discipline* "who opens and no one will shut, who shuts and no one opens" (Rev 3:7); and the width of his gate is precisely the measure of his wingspan upon the cross, precisely the gaping measure of the mouth of that garden tomb. Furthermore, for you who would enter this way and preach this way, for you who have humbly committed to conform your life to it, there is this marvelous promise, namely, that the one narrow way will ultimately lead not to one, but to twelve gates of pearl (Rev 21:21), gates that "will never be shut by day—and there will be no night there" (21:25); where the cantors and the choirs, the saints and the psalmists, and the angels themselves will be heard to sing, with all the architecture responding:

> Answer me when I call, O God of my right!
> You gave me room when I was in distress (Ps 4:1);

> He brought me out into a broad place;
> he delivered me, because he delighted in me (Ps 18:19);

> . . . you have set my feet in a broad place (Ps 31:8);

> . . . you have brought us out to a spacious place (Ps 66:11);

> Out of my distress I called on the LORD;
> the LORD answered me and set me in a broad place (Ps 118:5);

> I have seen a limit to all perfection,
> but your commandment [i.e., *your Word*] is exceedingly broad!
> (Ps 119:96)

O thanks be to God! O thanks be to God! To the blessed and only Sovereign, the King of Kings and Lord of lords, who alone has immortality and dwells in unapproachable light, be honor and eternal dominion. Amen.

§2. "Out of Context" OR "Subjective Reformation"[2]
(Isaiah 43:1–7; Psalm 107:1–3, 40–43; Luke 13:22–30)

PRAYER

You, O God, are the blessed and only Sovereign, and you alone have immortality and dwell in unapproachable light!

Since we cannot approach your light, let your unapproachable light approach us! Let it fall upon us like bracing waters, like the thunder of your cataracts, that we might be newly awakened and hear your deep calling unto our depths, that we might hear afresh your summons, and, when once we have examined ourselves and been examined, come again to your table. Amen.

Jesus went through one town and village after another, teaching as he made his way to Jerusalem. Someone asked him, "Lord, will only a few be saved?" He said to them, "Strive to enter through the narrow door; for many, I tell you, will try to enter and will not be able. When once the owner of the house has got up and shut the door, and you begin to stand outside and to knock at the door, saying, 'Lord, open to us,' then in reply he will say to you, 'I do not know where you come from.' Then you will begin to say, 'We ate and drank with you, and you taught in our streets.' But he will say, 'I do not know where you come from; go away from me, all you evildoers!' There will be weeping and gnashing of teeth when you see Abraham and Isaac and Jacob and all the prophets in the kingdom of God, and you yourselves thrown out. Then people will come from east and west, from north and south, and will eat in the kingdom of God. Indeed, some are last who will be first, and some are first who will be last." (Luke 13:22–30)

"(They) will come from east and west, from north and south, and will (sit at table) in the kingdom of God!" (v. 29) These are words we have grown accustomed to hearing in the invitation to the Lord's Table; at first glance, they seem such an obvious choice of text for Worldwide Communion.

---

2. World Communion Wednesday, October 1, 2008; Blades Chapel, University of Dubuque Theological Seminary.

Restored to their original setting, however, it becomes plain that our liturgy wrenches this verse rather wildly out of context. Instead of a reassuring, wide-open, all-inclusive, "feel good" invitation to the eschatological banquet, we have a finger-in-your-ribs warning, in which Jesus says: "Not only will 'not many' be saved, but you too will find yourselves shut out!" Little wonder the lectionary is afraid to approach this text! With our well-meaning questions about who will be saved and how many, we are simply not prepared to hear our Savior speak to *us* this way!

Why does Jesus seem to be so hard on those who simply ask concerning the salvation of others? Why is the Bible, generally speaking, so hard on religious professionals? These are questions that have troubled me for a long time, and if there is any place where they should be asked, a seminary setting, especially a seminary situated in the Reformed tradition, should be a fitting place in which to ask them.

How is it that you and I could find ourselves on the outside with the foolish bridesmaids, knocking, our way blocked by this owner of the house who speaks in this most intimidating fashion? Terrible as it is to consider, let us do just that. Let us do as it says in the text. Let us "begin to stand outside and to knock at the door, saying, 'Lord, open to us!'" Let's pluck up our courage and place our selves squarely in the sights of the Lord's rebuke in this passage. After all, is that not what the Reformed tradition is really all about: the reformation of sinners? Is it not about undergoing reformation for ourselves? Is it not the very reason the churches of the Reformation are known by the ubiquitous prayer of confession?

I say, let's be reformed! Knowing Jesus calls us to repent, let us remember that repentance is a gift from Christ himself (Acts 5:31); repentance itself is a grace, not a human work. *Sola gratia!* Only when we recognize that repentance is not a threat, but a gift, only then is it really *grace alone!* What is the worst that can happen, when the rebuke we are afraid to hear is actually a gift, a blessing in disguise?

What does Jesus rebuke here if not the selfsame tendency of those lawyers, who, having swiped the key of knowledge, "did not (themselves) enter (the kingdom), ... (and) hindered those who were entering" (Luke 11:52)? Jesus simply wants us to enter. And, by the way, not get in anyone else's way in the process. What does he rebuke if not our clumsy, objective blindness by which we see the crisis *outside* ourselves: "Lord, will only a *few* . . . of *them*, of *those folks out there* . . . be saved?"

"Yes," he says, "*many* will *try* to enter, but will not be able. Sadly, only a few will make it."

This is a terrible answer! Is it not! By which I mean, is it not terrifying? But, do not shrink, or slink, or slither away. That is what the brood of vipers do, those who are so earthbound and interwoven with their contexts that they cannot begin to sit up straight. Context, you see, derives from a weaving metaphor. And it is a perfectly fine metaphor, when we are speaking of literature, tapestries, robes, and stoles. But I am not convinced that "context" is the best word to use when we are speaking of complex human beings, relationships, cultures, and congregations, each of which surely deserve to be credited with living in four dimensions, or better yet, five! Least of all does the word context apply to what is going on in this meal, in which the real action is going on, not just down here, but up there! So do not shrivel at this tough word from Jesus. No, sit up straight, and listen, and remember that, as Peter says, "The Lord . . . is patient with you, not wanting any to perish, but all to come to repentance" (2 Pet 3:9).

Let us hold our ground, consider, and take courage in the fact that, to the Lord, even one lost sheep is worth pursuing; a flock of ninety-nine is too few when just one is missing. But "many, few, some," these are relative, quantitative terms.

Jesus has something else to say altogether, and he says it very directly. In fact, it is his terrible directness, his shift from the third person to the second, that thoroughly transforms the entire conversation from a hypothetical question about statistics and head counts—important as they are—into a mirror for self-examination: "Let's talk about you, little overseer. Who are you, 'little faith'? How did you come to be here? Are you a tourist in these parts? Are you lost? Where do you come from? O I know your so-called context, your spot on the map, for I was there, in the beginning, when every inch of this creation came into being; but it is your spiritual origin and your orientation that puzzle me. What are you doing out here? Are you a little son of thunder? No? A universalist? Well, wherever you are coming from, let me say what I said to my apostle: do not pronounce judgment—any judgment!—before the time, whether for good or ill . . .

> do not pronounce judgment before the time, before the Lord
> comes, who will bring to light the things now hidden in dark-
> ness and will disclose the purposes of the heart. (Only *then* will
> each one) receive commendation from God. (1 Cor 4:5)

Is it not dreadful to be thus addressed by the Lord? Is it not terrible to find our objective fig leaves so easily blown away when he turns from our speculative questions to this direct means of examination? "Who told you that you were naked?" (Gen 3:10).

Again, fear not. For in addressing us in this direct way, Jesus is giving us the very good, gracious and restorative gift of repentance that we need; he himself is turning us in the stiff wind of his Spirit. And how much more wonderful is *this* gift than the garments given to Adam and Eve! When he, our Sovereign, addresses us thus, it is to remind us that we are, as his human subjects, becoming fully human specifically in relation to his sovereignty, and thus we each begin to undergo the *subjective reformation* that is the essence of the Reformed tradition.

Put yet another way, Jesus, with this startlingly direct speech, puts in place the very "order of worship" of which Kierkegaard wrote when he reminded us that worship is *not* theatre, no, quite the oppo-site, and you, my friend, are not a spectator in the eyes of God. The audience in worship is a royal audience of One, and you and I are the ones under examination,[3] each of us passing beneath the staff of the one true Shepherd, through the sheep-gate, and on to the great feast that is spread before us. The preacher's job is simply to prompt you, to remind you that you are *part* of the choir, so to speak. You are no mere bystander, onlooker, overseer, tourist, critic, or "bean counter," but a full participant in the body of Christ. Seminary, church, ministry, kingdom of God: none of these are spectator sports, despite what Sunday means to the pagans!

Have we merely put a pleasant spin on this dreadful text? If you think so, think again. Think, for instance, of what the Spirit does with another dreadful text: the speech of a corrupt high priest, Caiaphas, that became (according to John) a prophecy of the highest and happiest order:

---

3. Kierkegaard, *Upbuilding Discourses in Various Spirits*, 122–25.

> You do not understand that it is better for you to have one man
> die for the people than to have the whole nation destroyed.
> (John 11:50)

So said the priest who orchestrated the death of our Lord. But before we condemn him, remember what the Spirit, speaking through the evangelist, has said:

> He did not say this on his own, but being high priest that year
> he prophesied that Jesus was about to die for the nation, and not
> for the nation only, but to gather into one the dispersed children
> of God. (John 11:51⁻52)

... to *gather into one* the dispersed children *of God.*

> Then (they, the children *of God*, those reformed subjects whose
> spiritual origin is *from above*, will arise out of their contextual
> enmeshments, and they) will come from east and west, from
> north and south, and sit at table in the kingdom.

So it will be for "them," but what about you and me? Well, lest you think the direct speech of the Lord is always so terrible, listen to what he says to "you" in the very words of which, I dare say, the hard saying of Luke 13 is the fulfillment, the very words that Jesus likely had in mind when he warned the gawking statistician to enter himself, and by *no other way* than himself, by no other way than the narrow gate, when he instructed you and me to not only to "try" the door, but to *strive* to enter, and to enter at all costs (v. 24):

> But now thus says the LORD,
> he who created you, . . . he who formed you, . . .
> Do not fear, for I have redeemed you;
> I have called you by name, you are mine.
> When you pass through the waters, I will be with you;
> and through the rivers, they shall not overwhelm you;
> when you walk through fire you shall not be burned,
> and the flame shall not consume you.
> For I am the LORD your God,
> the Holy One of Israel, your Savior. . . .
> Because you are precious in my sight,
> and honored, and I love you,
> I give (other) people in return for you,
> nations in exchange for your life.
> Do not fear, for I am with you;

I will bring your offspring from the east,
and from the west I will gather you;
I will say to the north, "Give them up,"
and to the south, "Do not withhold;
bring my sons from far away
and my daughters from the end of the earth—
everyone who is called by my name,
whom I created for my glory, whom I formed and made."
(Isa 43:1–7)

I owe it to you, and especially to my preaching students, to make the claim of this sermon as clear as possible, so here it is: The Reformed tradition is nothing, it is dead and irrelevant, if it is not first and foremost a fellowship in Christ of the joyfully repentant; Christ himself is handing this gift over to you, in Word and Sacrament; but all of these things: repentance as a gift and a joy, and fellowship with others who know it as such, require you to arise out of the supine flatness, the dust of your worldly contexts, and to step into a joyful, multi-dimensional awareness of life in God.

"Lord, will only a few be saved?" No, that is not the question. It is, rather, as though your Father in heaven is saying to you, "I know, child, I know. Numbers are important. But when it comes to worrying, why don't you let me worry about the numbers. You run along now and join the choir. You know the way. It's through the narrow gate. And remember, I formed you, I made you, I have redeemed you, I love you, and I will be listening for your voice as you sing!"

Bibliography

Achtemeier, Paul J. *Introduction to the New Hermeneutic*. Philadelphia: Westminster, 1969.

Barth, Karl. *Church Dogmatics. 1/1: The Doctrine of the Word of God*. Edited and translated by G. W. Bromiley and T. F. Torrance. Edinburgh: T. & T. Clark, 1936; 2nd ed., 1975.

———. *Church Dogmatics. 1/2: The Doctrine of the Word of God*. Edited and translated by G. W. Bromiley and T. F. Torrance. Edinburgh: T. & T. Clark, 1956.

———. *Church Dogmatics. 2/1: The Doctrine of God*. Edited and translated by G. W. Bromiley and T. F. Torrance. Edinburgh: T. & T. Clark, 1957.

———. *The Epistle to the Philippians*. Richmond, VA: John Knox, 1962.

———. *The Epistle to the Romans*. 2nd edition. Translated by Edwyn C. Hoskyns. London: Oxford University Press, 1968.

———. *The Göttingen Dogmatics: Instruction in the Christian Religion*. Vol. 1. Edited by Hannelotte Reiffen. Translated by Geoffrey W. Bromiley. Grand Rapids: Eerdmans, 1991.

———. *Homiletics*. Translated by G. W. Bromiley and D. E. Daniels. Louisville: Westminster John Knox, 1991.

———. *The Word of God and the Word of Man*. Translated by Douglas Horton. Gloucester, MA: Peter Smith, 1978.

Balthasar, Hans Urs von. *The Theology of Karl Barth*. Translated by John Drury. Garden City, NY: Anchor, 1972.

Beintker, Michael. *Die Dialektik in der 'dialektischen Theologie' Karl Barths*. Munich: Kaiser, 1987.

———. "Unterricht in der christlichen Religion." In *Verkündigung and Forschung: Beihefte zur "Evangelische Theologie,"* vol. 2, edited by Gerhard Sauter. Munich: Kaiser, 1985.

Braaten, Carl, and Robert W. Jensen, editors. *Either/Or: The Gospel of Neopaganism*. Grand Rapids: Eerdmans, 1995.

Breuninger, Christian. "Søren Kierkegaard's Reformation of Expository Preaching." *Covenant Quarterly* 51.3 (1993) 21–36.

Brown, Sally A. *Cross Talk: Preaching Redemption Here and Now*. Louisville: Westminster John Knox, 2008.

Bullock, Jeffrey. *Preaching With a Cupped Ear: Hans-Georg Gadamer's Philosophical Hermeneutics as Postmodern Wor(l)d*. New York: Lang, 1999.

Busch, Eberhard. *Karl Barth: His Life from Letters and Autobiographical Texts*. Translated by John Bowden. Grand Rapids: Eerdmans, 1994.

———. "Dialectical Theology." In *Encyclopedia of the Reformed Faith*, edited by Donald K. McKim, 100–102. Louisville: Westminster John Knox, 1992.

Buttrick, David. *A Captive Voice: The Liberation of Preaching*. Louisville: Westminster John Knox, 1994.

————. *Homiletic: Moves and Structures*. Philadelphia: Fortress, 1987.

Childers, Jana. *Performing the Word: Preaching as Theatre*. Nashville: Abingdon, 1998.

Childers, Jana, and Clayton J. Schmidt, editors. *Performance in Preaching: Bringing the Sermon to Life*. Grand Rapids: Baker, 2008.

Craddock, Fred B. *Overhearing the Gospel*. Nashville: Parthenon, 1978. 2nd ed. St. Louis: Chalice, 2002.

Dunning, Stephen N. "Paradoxes in Interpretation: Kierkegaard and Gadamer." In *Kierkegaard in Post/Modernity*, edited by Martin J. Matuštík and Merold Westfahl, 125–41. Studies in Continental Thought. Bloomington: Indiana University Press, 1995.

Ebeling, Gerhard. *Word and Faith*. Translated by James W. Leitch. Philadelphia: Fortress, 1963.

Friesen, Abraham. *Thomas Muentzer, A Destroyer of the Godless: The Making of a Sixteenth-Century Religious Revolutionary*. Berkeley: University of California Press, 1990.

Gadamer, Hans-Georg. *Philosophical Hermeneutics*. Translated by edited by David E. Linge. Berkeley: University of California Press, 1976.

————. *Truth and Method*. Translated by Joel Weinsheimer and Donald G. Marshall. New York: Continuum, 1997.

Gritsch, Eric W. "Luther, Martin." In *CEP* 315.

Hooke, Ruthanna B. "'I Am Here in This Room . . .'—The Practice of Performance and the Learning of Preaching." *Homiletic* 27 (2002) 13–21.

Ingalls, Jason T. "Review of William H. Willimon, *Conversations with Barth on Preaching*." Princeton: Center for Barth Studies, 2007. Online: http://libweb. ptsem.edu/collections/barth/reviews.aspx?menu=296&subText=468&disclaim er=668review.

Inwood, M. J. "Gadamer, Hans-Georg." In *OCP* 303.

Jeanrond, Werner. *Theological Hermeneutics: Development and Significance*. New York: Crossroad, 1991.

Kierkegaard, Søren. *The Book on Adler*. Vol. 24 of *KW*. Edited and translated by Howard V. Hong and Edna H. Hong. Princeton, NJ: Princeton University Press, 1998.

————. *Christian Discourses: The Crisis and a Crisis in the Life of an Actress*. Vol. 17 of *KW*. Edited and translated by Howard V. Hong and Edna H. Hong. Princeton, NJ: Princeton University Press, 1997.

————. *The Concept of Anxiety: A Simple Psychologically Orienting Deliberation on the Dogmatic Issue of Hereditary Sin*. Vol. 8 of *KW*. Edited and translated by Reidar Thomte and Albert B. Anderson. Princeton, NJ: Princeton University Press, 1980.

————. *The Concept of Irony with Continual Reference to Socrates*. Vol. 2 of *KW*. Edited and translated by Howard V. Hong and Edna H. Hong. Princeton, NJ: Princeton University Press, 1989.

———. *Concluding Unscientific Postscript to* Philosophical Fragments. Edited and translated by David Swensen and Walter Lowrie. Princeton, NJ: Princeton University Press, 1974.

———. *Concluding Unscientific Postscript to* Philosophical Fragments. Vol. 12 of *KW*. Edited and translated by Howard V. Hong and Edna H. Hong. Princeton, NJ: Princeton University Press, 1992.

———. *Eighteen Upbuilding Discourses.* Vol. 5 of *KW*. Edited and translated by Howard V. Hong and Edna H. Hong. Princeton, NJ: Princeton University Press, 1990.

———. *Either/Or I* and *II.* Vols. 3 and 4 of *KW*. Edited and translated by Howard V. Hong and Edna H. Hong. Princeton, NJ: Princeton University Press, 1987.

———. *Fear and Trembling/Repetition.* Vol. 6 of *KW.* Edited and translated by Howard V. Hong and Edna H. Hong. Princeton, NJ: Princeton University Press, 1983.

———. *For Self Examination: Judge For Yourself!* Vol. 21 of *KW.* Edited and translated by Howard V. Hong and Edna H. Hong. Princeton, NJ: Princeton University Press, 1990.

———. *The Moment and Late Writings: Articles from the* Fædrelandet; *The Moment; This Must Be Said, So Let It Be Said; Christ's Judgment on Official Christianity; The Changelessness of God.* Vol. 23 of *KW*. Edited and translated by Howard V. Hong and Edna H. Hong. Princeton, NJ: Princeton University Press, 1998.

———. *Philosophical Fragments; Johannes Climacus.* Vol. 7 of *KW.* Edited and translated by Howard V. Hong and Edna H. Hong. Princeton, NJ: Princeton University Press, 1985.

———. *The Point of View: On My Work as an Author; The Point of View for My Work as an Author; Armed Neutrality.* Vol. 22 of *KW*. Edited and translated by Howard V. Hong and Edna H. Hong. Princeton, NJ: Princeton University Press, 1998.

———. *Practice in Christianity.* Edited and translated by Howard V. Hong and Edna H. Hong. Vol. 20 of *KW*. Princeton, NJ: Princeton University Press, 1991.

———. *The Sickness unto Death: A Christian Psychological Exposition for Upbuilding and Awakening.* Vol. 19 of *KW.* Edited and translated by Howard V. Hong and Edna H. Hong. Princeton, NJ: Princeton University Press, 1980.

———. *Søren Kierkegaard's Journals and Papers.* Edited and translated by Howard V. Hong and Edna H. Hong. 7 vols. Bloomington: Indiana University Press, 1967–1978.

———. *Stages on Life's Way: Studies by Various Persons.* Vol. 11 of *KW*. Edited and translated by Howard V. Hong and Edna H. Hong. Princeton, NJ: Princeton University Press, 1988.

———. *Three Discourses on Imagined Occasions.* Vol. 10 of *KW*. Edited and translated by Howard V. Hong and Edna H. Hong. Princeton, NJ: Princeton University Press, 1993.

———. *Upbuilding Discourses in Various Spirits.* Vol. 15 of *KW*. Edited and translated by Howard V. Hong and Edna H. Hong. Princeton, NJ: Princeton University Press, 1993.

———. *Without Authority.* Vol. 18 of *KW*. Edited and translated by Howard V. Hong and Edna H. Hong. Princeton, NJ: Princeton University Press, 1997.

———. *Works of Love.* Vol. 17 of *KW.* Edited and translated by Howard V. Hong and Edna H. Hong. Princeton, NJ: Princeton University Press, 1995.

Leff, Gordon. *Heresy in the Middle Ages.* 2 vols. New York: Barnes & Noble, 1967.

Loder, James E. *The Logic of the Spirit: Human Development in Theological Perspective.* San Francisco: Jossey-Bass, 1998.

McCormack, Bruce. *Karl Barth's Critically Realistic Dialectical Theology: Its Genesis and Development (1909–1930).* Oxford: Clarendon, 1995.

———. "A Scholastic of a Higher Order: The Development of Karl Barth's Theology, 1921–1931." PhD diss., Princeton Theological Seminary, 1989.

Merrill, Timothy. "Interview with David Buttrick." Online: http://www.homiletics online.com/subscriber/interviews/buttrick.asp.

Migliore, Daniel L. "Karl Barth's First Lectures in *Dogmatics: Instruction in the Christian Religion.*" In Karl Barth, *DGD.*

Niebuhr, H. Richard. *Christ and Culture.* New York: Harper & Row, 1956.

Rottman, John M. "Performative Language and the Limits of Performance." In *Performance in Preaching: Bringing the Sermon to Life,* edited by Jana Childers and Clayton J. Schmidt, 67–86. Grand Rapids: Baker, 2008.

Schleiermacher, Friedrich. *Hermeneutics and Criticism and Other Writings.* Edited and translated by Andrew Bowie. Cambridge: Cambridge University Press, 1998. Originally published as *Hermeneutik und Kritik.* Edited by F. Lücke. Berlin, 1839.

Slemmons, Timothy Matthew. "Expand the Lectionary! The Need for and Features of Supplementary Year D." In *The Academy of Homiletics: Papers of the Annual Meeting, 42nd Mtg.* Minneapolis/St. Paul: Academy of Homiletics, 2007.

———. "Toward a Penitential Homiletic: Authority and Direct Communication in Christian Proclamation." PhD diss., Princeton Theological Seminary, 2004.

———. "*Synkrinesis* as Following in Faith: Interpretation for a Kerygmatic Homiletic." *KOINONIA* 13 (2001) 347–59.

Speickermann, Ingrid. *Gotteserkenntnis: Ein Beitrag zur Grundfrage der neuen Theologie Karl Barths.* Beiträge zur evangelischen Theologie 97. Munich: Kaiser, 1985.

Thiselton, Anthony C. *The Hermeneutics of Doctrine.* Grand Rapids: Eerdmans, 2007.

———. *New Horizons in Hermeneutics: The Theory and Practice of Transforming Bible Reading.* Grand Rapids: Zondervan, 1992.

Vos, Arvin. "Analogy." In *ERF,* 6–7.

Willimon, William H. *Conversations with Barth on Preaching.* Nashville: Abingdon, 2006.

Willimon, William H., and Richard Lischer, editors. *Concise Encyclopedia of Preaching.* Louisville: Westminster John Knox, 1995.

Name Index

Subject Index

Scripture Index

CPSIA information can be obtained at www.ICGtesting.com
Printed in the USA
LVOW10s1824180514

386296LV00026B/942/P